Term Limits

((Term Limits))

Gideon Doron and Michael Harris

LEXINGTON BOOKS
Lanham • Boulder • New York • Oxford

Dedicated to Becky Kook and Tali Harris,
and our children—Shira, Aeran, Batia, and Talia; Ron, Asaf, and Amit.

LEXINGTON BOOKS

Published in the United States of America
by Lexington Books
4720 Boston Way, Lanham, Maryland 20706

12 Hid's Copse Road
Cumnor Hill, Oxford OX2 9JJ, England

Copyright © 2001 by Lexington Books

British Library Cataloguing in Publication Information Available

Library of Congress Cataloging-in-Publication Data

Doron, Gideon.
    Term limits / Gideon Doron and Michael Harris.
        p. cm.
    Includes bibliographical references and index.
    ISBN 0-7391-0213-3 (alk. paper)
        1. United States. Congress—Term of office. 2. Term limits (Public office)—United
States. 3. Term limits (Public office)—United States—States. I. Harris, Michael, 1956-

JK1130 .D67 2001
328.73'073—dc21
                                                                                00-061938
Printed in the United States of America

⊖™ The paper used in this publication meets the minimum requirements of American
National Standard for Information Sciences—Permanence of Paper for Printed Library
Materials, ANSI/NISO Z39.48–1992.

Contents

Preface

Supreme Court judges are nominated for life because we want them to be able to decide cases as freely as possible from external and irrelevant pressures. Before they obtain their posts, their qualifications are thoroughly examined. Once chosen, they are provided with the proper conditions to minimize potential diversions from the subject matters under consideration. Because we accept and trust their moral integrity, most of us do not even know who these judges are. There are others, beside penitentiary dwellers, who seem to enjoy a life sentence in the public domain. Some head institutions of higher and lower learning; others stand at the top of governmental agencies. The Federal Reserve and the Federal Bureau of Investigation are two salient examples of agencies where the heads served for many years. The FBI's J. Edgar Hoover, for example, became an integrated part of the American public landscape. We justify these unusually long stays in public office on professional or other grounds. We do not ask to remove them from their posts because we are either satisfied with their performance or we do not understand or care enough. We feel uncomfortable, however, when such a lifetime occupation manifests itself in the political arena, when it becomes an undesired product of our choice.

A political phenomenon like Senator Strom Thurmon (R-South Carolina) is disturbing. He was born in 1902, was first elected in 1956, and has served in the Senate ever since. He is not the sole example, although he is unusual. Even in dictatorial regimes around the world, rarely does a politician last for so long in the public domain. Next to

Thurmon, one can recognize people like Robert C. Byrd (D-West Virginia) elected in the 1950s; Daniel K. Inouye (D-Hawaii) and Edward M. Kennedy (D-Mass.) elected in the 1960s; and Jesse A. Helms (R-North Carolina) and Joseph R. Biden (D-Delaware) elected in the early 1970s, among those who have spent most of their adult lives in the Senate. They reflect the essence of an interesting phenomenon at its extreme. In polities where no restrictions are set on the duration of people's service, elected or nominated to public offices, some may transform their conditional privilege into a lifetime occupation. This occurs at the national, state, and local levels of government.

Many people think that permitting politicians to occupy the public space for so long is wrong, that it leads to ineffective government and violates basic democratic values, and that the mechanism of periodic voting, designed to provide choices, is really a method to affirm earlier choices some of which were made many years ago under different political, social, and economic conditions. They have held that critical position since the early days of America's independence. Other people, including many office holders, see nothing wrong in these situations. They argue that the answer to the question of who should occupy political posts ought to be entirely the choice of the people to be expressed through free elections. Any attempt to affect these choices by external rules ought to be considered an attempt to temper with freedom, which is, after all, the highest value held by citizens in liberal democracies. The political, legal, institutional, and social manifestations of this argument, which materialized during the 1990s into a series of restrictions imposed on the length politicians can serve in elected office at the state level, is known as the term limit movement. The consequences of this movement's activities are the subject matter of this book.

The early 1990s witnessed major political changes around the globe. The Soviet Union, the principle ideological rival of the United States, had just collapsed, bringing to an end more than four decades of "Cold War." From the ruins of the old communist empire emerged the struggling democracy of Russia and several other independent republics. The Eastern bloc followed suit, beginning a long and painful process of democratization. The two parts of Germany united under one democratic flag, and established democracies like Italy, Japan, Australia, and Israel underwent major electoral reforms. Serious steps were taken in the European continent and, to a much lesser degree in the Far East, to bring down historical and legal barriers that prevented a more meaningful cooperation, at least on the economic level.

Naturally, all these reformers looked to the United States, whose stable political system seems to have been performing effectively for several generations, for a comparative example. From the outside it seemed at the beginning of the 1990s that except for electing a controversial president (Bill Clinton) in a three-man competition, very little political "newness" had been taking place in the United States. It looked as if America was essentially continuing to function as a two-party system, with a relatively high level of citizen's indifference and a very low turnout rate at election time. Some observers, however, identified the cause for this and other imperfections in the political system itself, a system designed to permit politicians to stay in office for an unlimited length of time. They argue that a long stay in office, in some cases more than thirty years, has been made possible because of, among other things, the relative competitive advantage incumbents hold in electoral races. Consequently, some observers, like Jack Yampolsky, went so far as to label the American political system as one that is dominated not by two parties but by one party—namely, the "incumbent party."

The internal change, which was followed by the dramatic success of the term limit movement at the state level, went almost unnoticed outside of the United States. It also drew little attention from states where the issue was not placed high on the public or political agendas or on the actual ballots on election day. But in almost half of the states the idea that politicians should not serve more than a specific length of time became a salient electoral issue directly affecting voters' choices.

It is interesting and important to note that the political reform of the 1990s did not originate with the politicians. In fact, most of the elected politicians opposed it, for the reform was directed at them. Perhaps the outcomes of the 1990s electoral races were too much for the people to take: 96 percent of the members of the House of Representatives were reelected, and many incumbents ran against no significant opponents.

To our knowledge, except for the work of Carey, Niemi, and Powell (1999), which mostly covers the actual effects of term limits at the state legislators' level, there is no systematic study on the term limits phenomenon and its applications and effects on American politics. Much of the relevant work on the issue was either published too early to be able to evaluate the nature and the magnitude of the change on American politics, or it was political in essence. Benefiting from the years that have passed since the initiation of the first sets of term limits in the early

1990s, we continue to examine the effects of the changes that were undertaken at the state level. We do that, however, from a different and a broader perspective. In passing we note that the relative lack of professional academic interest is, in our view, somewhat odd. Out of the many scholars who labor to explain the political phenomenon in general and in the United States in particular, few paid serious attention to what many considered the most important political reform of the American polity. It leads one to wonder why. We briefly deal with this question in the introduction.

In this book we study the logic underlying the idea of term limits and the effects associated with its implementation. We examine the idea as it was first proposed by the Founding Fathers, the political logic that guided the Supreme Court decision of 1995 regarding the constitutionality of state imposed term limits, and the practical developments and implementations of this idea at the state level. We also provide an in-depth account of one state—Michigan—to learn about the various nuances associated with the pro and con positions over this issue.

While we try as much as possible to stay neutral in the controversy that emerged over the adaptation of this idea on the national level, we often find ourselves siding with the proponents. As trained political scientists, our attempt to stay neutral means that we are not concerned with normative question of good or bad, nor with the question of who is right and whose argument is correct in this on-going debate. Yet it is easy to show, depending on a basic set of civic values and point of departure, and a sense of optimism or pessimism regarding the problem-solving ability of the political system, that every argument in favor can be matched by an equally convincing counter-argument. For us, questions of good or bad are relevant only insofar as they relate to the quality of the explanations offered. They are irrelevant for the assessment of the quality of political life in America, with or without term limits. Often, however, we are drawn to the side of the proponents of term limits and this is not always our intention. Our positive assessment of term limits is usually a result of the structure of the presented arguments; this is to say that the status quo, a state where politicians' terms of service is unrestricted, is known, and hence it needs not be explained much. The effect of the proposed change—term limits—is largely unknown and therefore deserves a fair treatment. Consequently, the analysis captures much of our sympathetic attention. We use our theoretical knowledge to explain why.

Several individuals helped us during our research and writings; they shared with us their time in interviews and wisdom in important suggestions that improved our understanding of the subject matter and the quality of the manuscript. Specifically, we would like to thank: Laurence N. Smith who initiated the idea for us to engage in the analysis of term limits. He would not let us rest until we decided to write the book and provided significant encouragement throughout the entire process. Luke Hennings, whose exhaustive research effort made this book possible. Kirk Profit, a former Michigan state legislator, played a major role in opening doors for us in Lansing, making it possible for us to meet with people who provided valuable insights for the book. Sharon Crutchfield is deeply appreciated for her support with editing, coordination and communication with all parties. Erin Emerine, Lisa Walters, and Marcy Lehtinen provided support with research, editing and coordination. We would like to thank several individuals who have collaborated with us over the years in research. They include, among others, Mark Daniels, Giora Goldberg, Ytzhak Katz, Barry Key, Rhonda Kinney, Becky Kook, Moshe Maor, Uri On, Don Peretz, Itai Sened, Martin Sherman, and Daniella Shonker. Our thanks go to two representatives from our publisher, The Rowman & Littlefield Publishing Group: Serena Leigh, for her belief in the value of the book, and Renee Jardine, whose editorial expertise was of profound assistance. Several friends were instrumental in providing a supportive environment: Barry Fish, Stuart Karabenick, Udi Lebel, Bernard O'Connor, Joe Rankin, Yaron Regev, and Ken Rusiniak. We would also like to thank Tel Aviv University, Eastern Michigan University, and Ben Gurion University for their generous support. Lastly, we would like to thank our wives—Becky Kook and Tali Harris; and our children—Shira, Aeran, Batia, and Talia; Ron, Asaf, and Amit, who bring true meaning to our lives. Their constant love and support has made this book possible.

Introduction

*Congress is never, not in a million years,
going to impose term limits on
itself—unless it has to.*

—Milton Friedman

Term limits is an idea rooted in classical republican thought. The principles that justify imposing limitations on the number of terms that legislators at the state and federal level may serve have been discussed since the early days of American political tradition. During the early part of the 1990s, these discussions, conducted in one form or another, resurfaced with great intensity, capturing the political agendas of about half of the American states. Proponents of term limits argue that the unfair advantages of the incumbency have adverse effects on the quality of the political life in America and consequently on our personal lives. Because it is very difficult to unseat incumbents, many citizens become indifferent and the motivation to vote is reduced. This is reflected in low turnout rates (most often less than 50 percent) in the races for federal level legislators and sometimes even a much lower rate in races for state legislators. Instead of serving as "citizen-legislators" as intended by the Founding Fathers and as expected by many of the voters, congressmen, senators, and state lawmakers have become "career politicians." Their actions are guided, as David Mayhew (1974) asserted, by an ever-existing attempt to maximize the probability of their reelection. By doing so, they often lose touch with their constituents. Years of working with lobbyists have made them the "puppets" of special interests, and with their support they are able to defeat any opposition. Given the freedom to run for office over and over again, these men and women are no longer true representatives of the people; they have became agents of their own greed and ambition.

These arguments and many corollary ones for term limits presumably struck a powerful chord with many people. Beginning in the 1980s, concerned citizens in various states organized themselves into movements with one clear message: limit terms for public representatives. Their efforts first bore fruit in 1990. In three states— Colorado, Oklahoma, and California—voters supported the ballot initiative to limit the terms of their state legislators. Five years later, nearly twenty states would pass various term limits in referenda, often by very large voting majorities.

The causes of the seemingly sudden popularity of the term limits movement have been the subject of much analysis. One of the commonly argued thoughts is that term limits represent the public's dissatisfaction with the state of politics in America. Term limits would then have not just a strong symbolic value, providing a sense of empowerment to otherwise powerless people (which is expressed in the oft-repeated slogan, "Throw the bums out!"), but also serves as an effective means of control of the people over their representatives. For people who believe that they have been long misguided by their representatives, term limits reflects a stand on principle rather than support of a position that guides their choices according to the quality of performance of their elected officials. This is one possible indication of a general mistrust or at least the prevalence of a serious problem that characterizes public perception regarding elected representatives at the state level.

It is easy to understand such a sentiment at the congressional level. Over the years, many people have become upset with the performance of Congress. The low turnout votes for congressional posts—especially in midterm elections, that place between presidential elections that still provides some political excitement—is a disturbing fact for any citizen. It became a matter of fact that congressmen do not represent majority choices any more. When fewer than half of the eligible voters participate in the usual two-person congressional race, then the winners would be, by definition, representatives of minorities. These minorities usually reflect the political power structure in a given state. They do not reflect the aspiration of the real minorities in the population, including women and members of various ethnic groups, whose practical access to power is blocked. The prevailing American political system sets very effective barriers to the entry of representatives of these minorities into the House and the Senate. Against the wishes of the Founding Fathers, Congress seemingly has become a secure fortress protecting itself from outside infiltration. It is not surprising, therefore, to find that women and minorities, underrepresented in Congress (as well as in many state legislators), support term limits in the hopes of seeing the likelihood of their representation increase. Consequently, politically sensitive and motivated women headed several of the state campaigns for term limits. In a study of the 1990 California Term Initiative, for example, Donovan and Snipp found that women were more likely than men to support term limits (Karp 1995:376).

What Ignited the Term Limits Movement?

Why has the idea of term limits been put on the states' agendas across the nation? Toward the end of the Bush administration, the state of the nation was not well. A poor economy with increasing numbers of unemployed and large budget deficits forced people to look to the government for solutions. But the inability of Congress (and the president) to identify and enforce a proper solution, coupled with several political scandals, led to a mere 17 percent public approval rating, an all-time low for that institution (Donovan and Snipp 1993; Jacobson 1993). In 1992, George Herbert Walker Bush lost his reelection bid to Bill Clinton. It is interesting, however, to consider how, in spite of this abysmal approval rating and such an unpopular Congress, so many incumbents were successful in seeking reelection. This we will examine later. For now suffice it to say that there is a great difference between disapproving of Congress in general and disapproving of one's own representative in particular; something that several incumbents have actually used to their advantage in reelection campaigns.

In other democracies, when the public disapproves of its representatives or it wishes to change the distribution of power in society, it can use several options. Short of a revolution, which changes the ideological nature of the polity, democratic societies may enact major or minor regime reforms. France, for example, enacted a major regime reform in the early 1960s. As a consequence of public demand to resolve the Algerian issue and the inability of the Fourth Republic parliament to deliver a solution, it moved to a presidential-type Fifth Republic (Rae

1967). In other places, such as Italy, Japan, or Israel, electoral reforms such as those enacted in 1992 are sufficient means to change the distribution of political power in the parliaments (Doron and Harris 2000). In most other democracies, the usual public response to unsatisfying political performance is done by founding new parties that compete in the election and can replace, if successful, the old ones.

All of these ways seem to be blocked for the American voters. It looks as if a change cannot come from within the political system. No one would seriously expect that Congress would vote itself out or enact legislation that would replace its members with new ones. Such action goes against the logic of political life. The proof is that politicians, regardless of the quality of their performance in Congress, stand again and again for reelection and win. So a change from the inside is highly unlikely. And, at least during the 1980s, there was no major national crisis of potentially catastrophic proportion that could affect the idea of a need for a major political change in the minds of most congressmen and congresswomen.

Therefore, if political change needs to occur, it must come from the outside, since Congress is obviously not going to do it and the other alternatives are not often employed by Americans. But change to the Constitution is a rare event.

No one seriously contests the supreme rule of the Constitution. It is the institution that provides considerable measures of stability to the American polity (Buchanan and Tallock 1962). Even in the early 1960s, when the civil rights movement was challenging governmental practices on all levels, its campaign was consistent with constitutional dictates (Kook 1992). Within its framework, introduction of amendments is an ever-existing option. But adding amendments is a very difficult task. Past attempts to introduce constitutional amendments opposed by the political system have failed. The most notable example is the Equal Rights Amendment (ERA) of the 1970s, which was aimed at providing women with explicit constitutional rights and protections. While at times women were able to bring state legislators to their side, this became more and more difficult as time passed. Finally, because of pressures from interest groups and other types of opposition, even state legislatures that had previously supported the ERA retreated from this position. Subsequently, the drive for the amendment was terminated, ending the expectations and hopes of many women (Mansbridge 1986).

The process by which amendments are introduced to the Constitution when Congress does not initiate them is designed to make it very difficult to obtain the required majority. It requires special majority consent among the states and, therefore, it is oriented toward the status quo and not political reforms. Nevertheless, constitutional amendments initiated by the people have been proposed and adopted over the years. Some, like the eighteenth amendment (prohibition of alcohol) passed through the entire system of security gates, even though the social costs associated with it were enormous. Riker and Ordeshook (1973) believe that no one was thinking at the time about the costs of enforcement associated with the amendment, or about the future consequences to societal norms brought about by a massive violation of the rule of law in America.

Amendments need not only come from the people. They can also be proposed through a Constitutional Convention (popularly known as Con-Con) called by the Congress on application of two-thirds of state legislators and ratified by conventions in three-fourths of the states. While this is an open option to introduce change that is specified in the Constitution, it is unrealistic. Its logic is contrary to the normal way of introducing amendments, so it has never been tried. It provides a mechanism for the public (i.e., state legislatures) to put effective dampers on "wild" congressional initiatives to introduce changes into the Constitution. For example, if Congress wishes to further limit the rights of the states, it is difficult to believe that it would be able to find enough support to form a Con-Con.

There is always the possibility of forming a third party, which would affect the outcomes in the desired direction. Third parties and independent politicians are always present in American politics (Abramson, Aldrich, Paolino, and Rohde 1995). More often than not their bids for effective power have been unsuccessful. The anti-Congress, anti-politics sentiments that led to the initiation of the term limit movement presumably fueled many voters' to support Ross Perot's formation of his Reform party and his unsuccessful bid for the presidency in 1992 and 1996.

A seemingly easier way to bypass internal opposition from both Congress and state legislators is the initiation of state movements. The target chosen is not a grand systemic change but a small internal one, merely to add another condition to the choice of the voters, to convince voters to support only those representatives who promise not only to serve the public (all do!) but those who will be sincere about it. And the way to assure the sincerity of the candidates' promise is to make it publicly known that for better or for worse, the number of terms of an elected official is limited. This idea could be brought to the public's attention in each state and, once accepted, it could affect the voters' calculus. Candidates who promise to serve only two or three terms would be favored among voters who support this idea. Candidates who do not make such promises would be at a disadvantage among such voters.

Since candidates tend to make promises during elections that they do not intend to fulfill, or they change their minds with the changing circumstances, the next stage is to formalize and institutionalize the promise: to make it clear to both voters and candidates that there is a binding contract between them. This kind of reasoning led to the propositions for the term limits laws in the three states mentioned earlier.

While citizens are free to determine the conditions underlying the service of their own state representatives, they may not be on the national level. This is because the relationship between the authorities of the state and the federal level of government are specified in the Constitution, and political decisions taken on one level but that affect the other level are problematic. A change on the federal level would entail a change to the Constitution, which, as we have demonstrated above, is extremely difficult. In 1995 the Supreme Court found that the limitation imposed on the number of terms of congressmen and congresswomen is unconstitutional. The analysis of this ruling will be discussed in chapter 2.

The Political Explanation

Changes do not occur in a vacuum. Organizational changes taking place in the political or other arenas are usually the products of entrepreneurs' labor (Doron and Sened 2001). There are individuals who are, in one way or another, likely to benefit from the outcome of the change. Therefore, in studying the effect the term limit movements have had on the American polity, one cannot ignore the question asked by the two notable sociologists Blau and Scott: "Cui Bono?" (Who benefits?) (1962:42) .

It may seem surprising to find out that the term limits issue became a major political item on the agendas of many Republican contenders. The issue of term limits is essentially a Democratic one, because it enables underrepresented minorities, most of who support the Democratic party, to enter into the political system. Indeed, several Democrats felt that the issue had been "stolen" from them by the Republicans. Not so. A cynical or, rather, practical view of politics explains why not. We present it briefly here and develop it further in chapter 3.

Electoral competition is affected by many factors that can be summarized into three groups: voters' identification with the party; the issue position of the candidates; and the personality (real or perceived) of the candidates (Doron 1988). The Democrats are traditionally the largest American party, with many more registered members than the Republicans. The issue positions of candidates competing in the various states and endorsed by the two parties are usually very similar. That is, in the conservative South both candidates would support conservative positions, and in the liberal North they would usually support liberal issues. It must be so, if the candidates aim to win congressional election and are not merely interested in "showing" the voters their sincere position. A winning strategy requires candidates to hold a median position, one in which at least half of the voters support (Brams 1985). When both candidates hold similar positions, then what matters to the voters are their personalities. Here, incumbents have an advantage because they are usually better known than their challengers, so supporting them entails less risk.

On these three counts, at least in the last five decades, the Democrats have fared better than Republicans in the races for the House of Representatives. In fact, they held solid majorities in the House from 1952 to 1994. How could one change these facts without compromising much on ideology and on the social composition of the party? The answer to this strategic question is: flush out to the surface the personality factor. Many Republicans, eager for their party to gain congressional control, pushed for the enactment of term limits at the federal level. The issue of term limits thus did not affect the regular party's issues, nor did it change party loyalty (except for the activists who committed themselves to support proponents of the proposition), but it forced out incumbents, thus opening up the possibility of a fair competition between two new contenders. Republican candidates were thus able to equalize their competitive chances and consequently increase their numbers in the House.

But even if that were exactly the grand political strategy of the Republicans, decided in the smoke-filled back rooms of the nation's capital, few would admit to it. No one would presumably support a proposition that provides advantages to candidates on technical grounds. Such an idea, political in essence, must be marketed to the public packaged by substantive reasoning and normative lingo. This had been produced in abundance. George Will, for example, the renowned spokesman for conservative causes, supplied, in a series of syndicated articles and a well-publicized book, enough arrows against the prevailing status quo. This book, *Restoration: Congress, Term Limits and the Recovery of Deliberative Democracy* (1991), suggested that term limits would not just bring Congress "closer to the people," an inherently populist ambition. Rather, it would, as Will argued using the words of Harvey Mansfield, "open some constitutional distance between the electorate and its representatives, the better to encourage a more deliberative legislative life" (Will 1997). Obviously, such messages were accepted by many because they touched real issues concerning the relationship that exists between the citizens and their political representatives. These issues include accountability, transparency, sensitivity, and responsiveness, and they are associated not only with the term limits concept but also with the quality of the political life in America. The political formula became quite simple: because representatives serve the public for longer than they should, the quality of their performance, as defined by the above-mentioned attributes, is not up to par. A shorter span of service would therefore bring them back to the public domain as it should be and as it was intended by the Founding Fathers. Indeed, a proposition for political reform and innovation in the theory and practice of government was articulated as a conservative legacy.

The 1995 Supreme Court ruling (see chapter 2) did not kill the initiative, although it slowed it down considerably. However, once the term limits concept was out, capturing the public and the political agendas, it affected voters' calculus and presumably would continue to be taken into consideration. Since the court ruling, the arena has shifted completely to the state level. Economic conditions, collectively and personally, improved considerably during Clinton's presidency; more Republicans than before entered the House after 1994; and mobilization of supporters in "new" term limits states has become somewhat more difficult. Hence, much of the original excitement associated with the movement has dissipated.

Political Science and Term Limits

Imagine a situation in which the government, or for that matter a nationally organized movement of concerned citizens, pushes for a change in the income tax rate and proposes to fix it 10 percent higher than it presently is. In such a not-so-hypothetical case, one would expect that the members of the professional community of economists would comment on the matter, providing academic, not to say scientific, evaluation of the proposed change. This expectation is based on a simple fact: that is what economists usually do. Note that the proposed change is one within the existing tax system; it is not a "revolutionary" proposal to reform the system itself. Note also that no one expects the community of learned economists to say whether the increase is good or bad; this they can do as concerned citizens.

Now consider the idea of term limits. It is a proposal for a major political change, which has already been enacted in some places. It could have a significant effect on the working of the American government. It is therefore expected that political scientists, like the economists in the case mentioned above, would bring out their professional tools and assist voters and politicians in their assessment of the nature of the choices they should make regarding term limits. On the contrary, for example, when an important book was edited (e.g., Grofman 1996) based on a conference that was held in 1991 at Irvine, California, on the topic, it was marketed as follows: "Political scientists and economists predict the consequences of legislative term limits at the state and national levels, *not in order to influence the current debate but to allow the next generation of scholars to evaluate the theories and methods of predictions,*" as if the knowledge accumulated by political scientists is relevant only to themselves. Surprisingly, most political scientists and the profession as a whole were relatively idle on the term limit issue. Less than a handful of books (see bibliography), a sporadic conference here and there, a representative panel in a scientific meeting (e.g., 1999 Annual meeting of American Political Science Association), some articles in journals, and a few commentary appearances in the written and electronic media, could sum up the entire professional contribution. Those among the prominent political scientists who were asked to voice their opinion on the issue were usually boldly against it at either the federal or state level.

Mark Petracca, a long time proponent of term limits, tried to explain "why political scientists oppose term limits" (1992a). But the illustrations he brings for professional opposition have less to do with the science of politics than with politics itself. The distinguished scholars do not offer their evaluation; they tell the people what they think. Nelson Polsby, for example, calls term limits "[a] constitutional mischief"

(1991a); Cronin says that "[it is] an illusory quick-fix for a symptom" (1990); Baker thinks that "[it is a] quack therapy for democracy" (1990); and Ornstein goes as far as saying that "[the] bums will rule" after the implementation of term limits (1990). Perhaps the mildest criticism comes from Mann, who simply believes that the use of term limits is "basically antidemocratic" (1979). Mann was among the first to systematically address this issue.

Petracca offers six considerations to explain this bold opposition, including the following. As professional political scientists advocate and identify themselves with the increased professionalism of the state legislators, they fear that term limits will encourage participatory democracy, and this will adversely affect stability and efficiency. They are cynical about the voters' ability to make the right judgements, and they are committed to the conservation of leadership. They believe that term limits are a threat because it goes against the ethos of academic professionalism. Last, they oppose it because term limits is perceived as being essentially a Republican issue, and many of them are Democrats.

Perhaps Petracca is exaggerating, and there are some professional reasons for the silence. One can think of other explanations for such a position. For example, many political scientists are, in fact, historians in training; term limits is a current event. Hence, it is lacking the perspective of a retrospective learned analysis. Likewise, many of the scholars are quantitatively oriented, and there has not yet been enough data accumulated to assess the effect of term limits on the state legislators. In this respect, the work of Carey (1998) and Carey, Niemi, and Powell (1999) on state legislators, or the research of Marckini, Strat, and Rader (1999) and of Sarbaugh-Thompson and Thompson (1999), among others, concerning the implementation of term limits in the state of Michigan, could be taken as some indications of a future trend. These works show a careful approach to the subject matter. Comparative experts have little to say on the matter of term limits. Most democracies have not implemented the policy of term limits for their own legislators. Those countries that impose limits on their representatives, like Costa Rica, Ecuador, the Philippines, and even Mexico, are not very interesting or very important to most American students of politics (Carey 1998). Certainly, it is difficult to imagine that American experts would see them as models of functioning democracies to be imitated. In addition, formal theorists, especially the neo-institutionalist group, who labor to identify local and general political equilibrium, would get little benefit from examining the effects of term limits. They are engaged in specifying the effects of institutions (like the American Constitution or the two-party system) that induce stability (e.g., Shepsly and Weingast 1981). Term limits, at least in the foreseeable future, would most likely create a destabilizing effect (see more in chapter 3).

There may be a different explanation, one that relates to the essence of political research. Here is a possible speculation. As in any attempt to interpret real world evidences, scholars can identify only those items that their professional and disciplinary eyeglasses direct them to. Gradually, the political phenomenon, the subject matter of research, becomes the thing itself. It is long forgotten that politics in general, and democracy specifically, are but methods used by people for the betterment of their lives. Political scientists, like the economists who see the world through the economic prism, also see their surroundings through professional filters. And the prospects shown by the supporters of term limits are not very appealing. They talk of democracy that is not functioning well and not serving well, that political stability is obtained at very high costs, paid by people who are located outside of the political game. They show that populist tendencies and drives may be very effective, that a change, a dramatic one, may affect the political system, making their explanations and predictions somewhat irrelevant. In some sense, term limits may affect the personal position of the professional; therefore, it is either rejected or ignored.

Last, public policy analysts can say little on this matter. The policy of term limits has been implemented without being tested first by one or another experimental design whose effects could be evaluated. Hence, the political science community as a whole was neither prepared for nor had the tools to professionally comment on the dramatic ongoing event in the American polity of the 1990s. It will no doubt focus more attention on the issue as time passes.

This book is divided into two parts. In the first part we analyze the concept of term limits as it manifests itself on the national level. The first chapter deals with the initiation of the concept by the Founding Fathers and its historical evolution. We examine the intentions and the line of reasoning used by the concept's proponents like James Madison, and contrast it with that of their opponents, most notably Alexander Hamilton. We also make the important distinction between the controversial limitations imposed on the number of terms of legislators and of the accepted limitations imposed on members of the executive branch of government: that is, presidential term limits.

The second chapter analyzes the 1995 Supreme Court ruling on *U.S. Term Limits, Inc., et al. v. Thornton et al.* This ruling, which was decided by a five to four call, prohibits states from setting restrictions on the number of terms representatives may serve in the U.S. Congress. Admittedly, our sentiments lie with the minority position but for several other reasons that are developed in the third chapter. Based on the accumulated theoretical knowledge in the discipline of political science, the chapter addresses several concepts that should be clarified before an analysis of the controversy and the assessment of the effects of the term limits law takes place. These include the notions of the power of the incumbent; the nature of the legal and practical barriers to entry into political systems; the real "freedom" people have in their choices; and the relationship between what people want and what they actually get in the political sphere.

The second part of the book concentrates on the implementation of the term limits laws at the state levels. Chapter 4 compares the activities of the particular term limits movements operating in each of the various states that adopted term limits during the early 1990s. It also provides updated comparative reports on three interesting term limits' states: California, Colorado, and Massachusetts. Against this descriptive background, chapter 5 analyzes, from both the political economy and organizational theory perspectives, the expected effects of limiting the number of terms a legislator may serve in his or her state congress and on the quality of public policymaking in that state and in general. Several topics are analyzed in this chapter, including the effects of experience, efficiency, and effectiveness, and the element of time in the context of term limits.

Chapter 6 concentrates on one state as a case study for in-depth analysis. We chose for that purpose the state of Michigan, because it is more or less an "average" state, and also because one of us has an open access to this state's policy and lawmaking process.

In the conclusion we ask a simple question: does it really matter? Are we engaged in a real reform in the American polity, which carries important substantive consequences for society, or is the whole thing another political scheme designed to effect personnel changes on the state level and in Washington? We believe and show that term limits is a major internal reform in the American political system and that its effects have already been internalized, changing the way voters perceive politics.

Part One

THE CONSTITUTIONAL DILEMMA

Controversy over term limits has taken several routes. Among them, one is related to the federal level of government and the other to the state level. Within each level there is a distinction between the executive and the legislative branches. It seems that most people accept the formal and actual division: that executive term limits are beneficial, while the legislative-type term limits are problematic. It also seems that most people accept the right of the states to limit the terms of service of the representatives to their own institutions of government, while they are not so convinced that the same right should be granted to states wishing to restrict the terms of their representatives to the U.S. Congress.

Part One, which consists of three chapters, presents the problematic nature of term limits as it applies to the federal level of government. The first chapter traces the historical evolution of the idea. It distinguishes between legislative and executive term limits. The second chapter analyzes the 1995 Supreme Court decision to prohibit states from imposing limits on their representatives to the U.S. Congress. This ruling brought to the forefront the old issue of state vs. federal rights and made a strong case for the latter. In chapter 3 we go to the theoretical board. In the context of federal term limits we explain the meaning of concepts such as "free choice," "majority choice," "incumbency," and "barriers to entry," all used by proponents and opponents of the term limits idea, as it was intended to be applied to the federal level.

Chapter One

The Origins and Evolution of Term Limits

*Politicians in government should be changed
regularly, like diapers, for the same reason.*
—Richard Davies, Geneva, Switzerland

While the guiding political wisdom in tyrannies often advises against replacing a veteran dictator with a new one because, as the saying goes, "the starving new one would quickly and rapidly move to exploit the people," replacement of politicians is a central attribute of democracies. The mechanism of popular election is designed to allow the public to determine representation and ideas. Regimes that do not offer the option of replacement through periodic elections cannot be considered democracies. This is so basic that even dictatorships of the communist version (i.e., "People's Democracies") or the authoritarian kind (e.g., Islamic theocracies or military regimes) are careful to conduct periodical elections. No one is really being replaced by these elections, but their leaders can claim that they are sensitive and attuned to the public wishes, and that these elections reconfirm the fact that they are the true representatives of the "people's choice."

Were elections an efficient mechanism for replacement, the issue of term limits would probably not have surfaced. Term limits do not affect the tenure of ideas, only the duration of public service of the people who express them. But once surfaced, term limits assumed other merits. The debate over its essentiality to the management of public life emerged because to adapt it means to forego other values that seemed beneficial to the conduct of one's polity. Hence, a controversy over the social and individual costs versus benefits that may result from the implementation of term limits developed into an area of immeasurable values. The usual way to settle such controversy in democracies is through the political process: legislation, voting, or simply raising it to public attention, thus affecting people's preferences. This was done in the 1990s.

In this chapter we trace the evolution of the term limits idea since ancient times. Special emphasis is given to the position held by the American Framers of the Constitution. We distinguish between the requirement to restrict the terms of the legislators and to limit the terms of the executives. We argue that the logic underlying these two demands is quite different, although both proponents and opponents often use a line of reasoning that is proper for one branch of government to make a point for the case regarding the other branch.

A Democratic Imperative

Perhaps the first Western source reflecting the tension that exists between the concept of holding a permanent public position and favoring the imposition of time limits is found in the Old Testament story of how Saul was anointed king. There, it is told, the Hebrews came to Samuel, their undisputed spiritual leader, asking him to appoint them "a king to govern [us], like the other nations." Until then the Hebrews were ruled by periodic leaders, called Judges. When their security was threatened, a person of leadership quality—a member of one of the twelve tribes—was asked to lead a campaign against the enemy. Once victory was obtained "and the land became pacified" again, that person would return to his (and in the case of the Judge Deborah—her) old occupation: a farmer or a shepherd or whatever. Samuel could not reject his people's request (1 Sam., 8.11-18), but he warned them that choosing a permanent leader, a king, would result in tyrannical conduct. They would have to pay dearly to that king: "He will take your sons and make them serve in his chariots and with his cavalry. . . . He will take your daughters for perfumers, cooks and confectioners. . . . He will take one tenth of your grains and your vintage . . . and you yourselves will become his slaves." But the Hebrews were not convinced. He then anointed Saul, a member of the smallest Hebrew tribe, Benjamin, to become the first king of Israel.

Protection against tyrannical unrestricted conduct is a major theme that became pivotal in the thinking of prominent British philosophers. It also significantly affected the thinking of the Framers of the American Constitution. It is not, however, the only major theme associated with periodical ruling. The ancient Greeks, the ideological rivals of the Hebrews, had another interpretation. Athens, which was governed by a mechanism of direct democracy, limited the terms of its public officials. During the fifth century B.C.E., for example, the Athenians selected their council annually with the provision that no one could serve on it for more than two years in his lifetime. Indeed, Aristotle, the great Greek philosopher, had listed term limits, or rotation, as one of his constitutional features of democracy, demonstrated by the principle of "ruling and being ruled in turn" (Petracca, 1992b:20).

For Aristotle, and many others who followed his normative dictates, ruling ought to be considered a civic duty, a service to the public, performed for a designated amount of time in the political arena. This is similar to the modern jury duty, which requires citizens to become "judges" at least once in their lives and for a very short time. Citizens' experience with ruling is important for the proper development of public sensitivities and responsibilities. It is therefore good and leads to a better state.

This notion was echoed many years later by Benjamin Franklin, who wrote: "In free governments, the rulers are the servants, and the people their superiors and sovereigns. For the former therefore, to return among the latter [is] not to degrade but to promote them" (U.S. Term Limits 2000). To date, in many small voluntary associations, and in particular in the Israeli political construction known as Kibbutz, where decisions are undertaken by means of direct democracy, periodic rotation in the chairmanship post is a guiding principle (Peretz and Doron 1997). The Swiss presidency also follows this rule of rotation (Rae 1967; Powell 1982).

Like Samuel before him, the German philosopher Immanuel Kant was concerned with the consequences of tyrannical rule. He believed that there is nothing safer than a "republican" regime because it has a constitution, which is based on the principle of freedom, dependence on a single legislation, and equality of the members (Kant 1963:94-95). Hence, these three conditions are favorable to the prospect for "perpetual peace." In contrast: "In a constitution which is not republican, and under which the subjects are not citizens, a declaration of war is the easiest thing in the world to decide upon, because war does not require the ruler . . . the least sacrifice of the pleasures of his table . . . he may therefore resolve on war as on a pleasure party for the most trivial reasons" (Kant 1963:95)

The fundamental question of who should bear the costs of collective action and for what reasons could not escape the English and Scottish political thinkers of the seventeenth and eighteenth centuries. They were well-versed in Biblical knowledge, Aristotelian reasoning and, of course, European thoughts. They were familiar with their former Greek justification of imposing term limits on rulers. Unlike Aristotle, however, they did not see rotation as a means of educating and developing virtues in the citizenry, nor as a way to improve the conduct of the state. Most of them held a rather negative view of government, expected little from it, and warned about its potential misconduct. Among them, the two liberal philosophers, John Locke and James Harrington, believed that to protect against the infringement of individual liberties, one should design effective checks against tyrannical ambitions. Protection of the rights of the individuals, not the betterment of the mechanism of the state and its citizenry, is the ultimate goal of politics. The issue of term limits, because of its relation to fundamental questions of how we choose to govern ourselves, became one such mechanism for protection.

Not all liberal thinkers sided with this view. The modern debate over term limits most likely emerged with the criticism of Harrington's *Commonwealth of Oceana* (1656). David Hume, in "Idea of a Perfect Commonwealth" (1752), argued that term limits were inefficient and unnecessary. He believed that the idea of removing office holders regardless of their performance and forcing a new set of lawmakers to learn political and legislative processes without the benefit of experienced and knowledgeable lawmakers should be rejected. That is consistent with the principles of fairness and common sense; for the benefit of public interest, good ruling behavior should be rewarded or at least not stopped. Otherwise we would confront unavoidable political instability generated by inexperienced legislators.

But what about bad ruling behavior? How can we defend ourselves against an abuse of power? How can we minimize the adverse effects of what Alexander Hamilton, Hume's most prominent American follower, considered almost a universal law, observing that: "A fondness of power is implanted in most men, and it is natural to abuse it when acquired" (Hamilton et al. 1991:103-104)). Hume's criticism of term limits set off a debate between two opposing groups of liberal republicans, a debate that would continue through the founding of America and to which we now turn.

Setting Up the Rules: Congressional Term Limits

Revolutions, major national catastrophes, and wars of independence are events that provide the best opportunities to set up new rules for the future conduct of a polity (Braybrook and Lindblom 1963). These rules naturally reflected the quality of the Framers' interpretations of their present conditions, including the prevailing political culture, their visions for the future of the polity, and the products of their interpersonal disagreements. The American Constitution was framed on the basis of intellectual and practical experience and with a profound vision. It was designed against a bad collective memory of British rule.

The British government had ruled the American colonies from across the Atlantic Ocean. Its primary concern was Great Britain, not the people in the colonies. By geography and manner of governance, the rulers were too far separated from the colonies for any chance of responsive ruling. Because colonists felt that they had lived under tyrannical rule where colonial governors seemed aloof and uncaring about the people for whom they were responsible, much revolutionary discourse was devoted to the need to ensure that this situation would not repeat itself. Or as Thomas Paine put it: "[that] the elected might never form to themselves an interest separate from the electors" (Paine 1776). Fearful of their new government once again becoming a legislative aristocracy, early Americans viewed term limits as one way of preventing the government from becoming too remote from the people. Paine was most paranoid on matters of power and its abuse. He writes:

> Men who look upon themselves as born to reign, soon grow insolent . . . their minds are already poisoned by importance . . . the world they act in differs so materially from the world at large . . . and when they succeed to government they are frequently the most ignorant and unfit of any. (1776)

Consequently, the Articles of Confederation included term limits for representation in Section V, which stated that no congressman "Should be capable of being delegate for more than three years in any term of six years." John Adams, Benjamin Franklin, and Thomas Jefferson, among others, supported the principle of term limits. For them, it seemed to be a natural and inevitable part of modern republicanism, an excellent device for guarding against accumulation of excessive power, corruption, and complacency of those elected to office. Six years later, however, the new United States Constitution did not include any provisions for the automatic removal of an elected official. What caused a complete reversal and rethinking of the necessity of term limits as a proper check against potential power abuse? A reversal in attitudes, so it seems, that generated a continuous debate, one which has still not been settled.

The declining support for term limits roughly correlates with the decline of the Articles of Confederation; perhaps there is even somewhat of a causal link. Some delegates to the Continental Congress, fond of their new political position, refused to abide by the dictates of Section V. Thus, for example, in 1784, when the three-year term for delegates expired, representatives from Rhode Island refused to leave office without a struggle. Others, some the most popular members, were forced to leave office. Consequently, the Republican Society sided with the opposition and aggressively attacked the concept of term limits as being "antidemocratic" because people were "deprived of the right of choosing those persons whom they prefer" (Petracca 1992b:30). Present-day politics reflect the same phenomenon. Once in power, people will go far to sustain their positions, even breaking their initial promises that helped them to taste the fruits of power in the first place. Scott McInis, for example, a Colorado representative, broke his promise in 1998 to voluntarily limit his congressional tenure. He is not the exception.

Despite a very difficult time for the young republic (1781-1787), which saw a system of government collapse and many of its attendant features attacked, the notion of term limits had not completely lost its appeal. Edmund Randolph of Virginia submitted term limits as part of a plan to the Constitutional Convention in 1787. Other members, including Rufus King and Nathaniel Gorham of Massachusetts, supported the idea. A year later, Gilbert Livingston of New York proposed that U.S. senators be limited to six years in office in any twelve-year period. Indeed, an intensive debate over the issue emerged between the Federalists and the Anti-Federalists.

Most of the distinguished Framers, proponents of the notion, continued to hold onto their initial positions. Alexander Hamilton, however, became the most known and indeed the best articulator of the opposition to term limits. John Adams, a supporter, could not retreat from his original position and continued to believe (as cited in Benjamin and Malbin 1992:26):

> Elections, especially of representatives and counselors, should be annual, there not being in the whole circle of the science a maxim more inflexible than this, "where annual election end, there slavery begins." These great men should be [chosen]

once a year like bubbles on the sea of matter bourne, they rise, they break, and to the same return. This will teach the great political virtues of humility, patient, and moderation, without which every man in power becomes a ravenous beast of prey.

Against this, Hamilton, who was taking a completely intransigent stand against all anti-Federalist positions regardless of their worth, brought David Hume to support his new position. Hamilton echoed Hume in opposition to term limits as well as a proposal for recalling senators in mid-term, stating that there should be "a principle of strength and stability in the organization of our government." To obtain this he went far, adding that he wanted more than just the absence of term limits: he wanted the U.S. Senate to be a "permanent body" that would "hold its authority during considerable period" (Malbin, as cited in Benjamin and Malbin 1992:59). Indeed, he and the other Federalists, fearing the "tyranny of the majority," wanted more than just a representative body that would serve as a funnel for the wishes of its constituents. They wanted an institution that could withstand populist pressures and temptations. A permanent body could better serve the public good if the representatives were given considerable power; to limit the amount of time a legislator might serve would make him less regardful of the public and more susceptible to corruption. The British House of Lords comes closest to this model of the Senate. The conditions proposed are similar to those provided to Supreme Court judges to protect their integrity and freedom of choice.

Perhaps the best expression of this radical idea from the point of view of the Federalist republicans was made by Richard Harrison (Benjamin and Malbin 1992:59) during the New York debate over term limits:

> [If a legislator] knows that no meritorious exertions of his own can procure a reappointment, he will become more unambitious, and regardless of the public opinion. The love of power, in a republican government, is ever attained by a proportionable sense of dependence.

Interestingly, the arguments in favor of term limits expressed in the 1990s often refer to what the Federalists argued in opposition to term limits: legislators becoming corrupt, distancing themselves from their constituents, and becoming less and less concerned with the public interest. The Federalists, favoring a strong central government with no term limits, preferred the U.S. Senate to be composed of men whose knowledge, ability, and experience were necessary for the proper functioning of the political and legislative processes. Today, an advocate of term limits might refer disparagingly to such persons as "career politicians."

But they were not. And this is presumably the prime political explanation for why term limits were not included in the constitution, even in reference to the executive branch. Because of the prevailing political culture, term limits became unnecessary. The Federalists could "give" this issue to the anti-Federalists. Many of the congressmen saw themselves as volunteers in the service of their states and nation. They also believed that the proper thing to do was to let others volunteer too. Thus they frequently left their offices in the state legislatures and, as John Fund notes, about 40 percent of House incumbents did not seek reelection and returned to their homes following Washington's first election to the presidency (as cited in Benjamin and Malbin 1992:227). Moreover, delegates at the Philadelphia Convention agreed to set short terms of office for both the president and members of Congress, precluding the necessity for term limits. In general, most did not exclude them because they saw such limits on the executive and the legislature as somehow unhealthy for the new republic; they were not seen as terrible evils to be avoided. At most they were seen as unnecessary safeguards for issues sufficiently dealt with by other provisions.

Indeed, the culture of voluntary rotation that prevailed among the legislators was validated, if not reinforced, by Washington's departure after only two terms in office (a presidential practice that continued until FDR; see below). This guided the normative standard of behavior. Petracca supports this point. He too sees the self-imposed rotation that prevailed among national legislators even by those luminaries of the U.S. Congress whose cumulative service in elected office was quite lengthy, such as John Calhoun, Daniel Webster, and Henry Clay, as the guiding political norm in the land (1992b:37-38). The fact is that over the years and especially during the twentieth century, this norm of voluntary rotation, which well defines the concept of citizen-legislator, has eroded. This concept has been replaced, as modern proponents of term limits argue, by the norms and standards of political careerism and the power of the incumbency. The reasons for this gradual replacement should be attributed to many factors. Prime among them are some very practical ones that are not necessarily related to a devotion to some principle, such as the improved conditions of a congressman's stay in Washington.

At the time, the American capital was located in the middle of nowhere, just as the capitals of some other modern countries, such as Brasilia in Brazil, are located far from the locus of their country's concentration of people. When the railroad system was yet to be developed and efficient cars more than a century from being invented, getting to Washington D.C. was certainly not a pleasant task. Travel to and from congressmen's homes to the capital was arduous. In addition, congressmen found it difficult not only to reach Washington D.C., but also to stay there for very long (Kamber, Hyden, and Gephardt 1995:26-27). There was very little to do in Washington except for politicking, and congressmen received very little or no pay for their work there. It was also difficult because they could not take effective care of their political bases at home nor of their personal economic business. Few could use their positions to advance their personal welfare because at the time the prevailing ideology kept the government at a necessary minimum. People who were not blessed with resources before they assumed their political responsibilities could not therefore stay in such a situation for long, even if they were driven by great psychological motivation to serve the public. So they quit, either because they wished to return to their business or because, as a consequence of their long stay in Washington, they saw an erosion in their home power bases and hence no chance of being reelected. Thus, one or two terms of service were considered by many to be enough.

Things have changed over the years, of course. Payments for public officials have improved considerably. Access to and from Washington has become easy, quick, and comfortable, by trains, cars, and jet planes. And the city has turned into one of the most important cultural centers of the United States, if not the world. Under these and other attractive conditions, it is no wonder that politicians are drawn to that place and, once there, invest much effort to maintain their position. George Will (1997b) provides some figures: America's median household income in 1995 was a bit over $34,000. The average income was about $45,000. The congressional salary was $133,600, up from $75,000 in 1984. Only six members of the seventy-three freshmen elected to the House in 1996 got lower pay than they had been making in their previous jobs. Only a few reject the temptation to stay for more. For example, Rep. Elizabeth Furse (D-Oregon) decided in 1977 not to seek reelection for the fourth term stating, "It is a tremendous strain for people who live in the West Coast. My family is in Oregon. I have a two-year-old grandson and I want to get to know him real well" (*Washington Post* 17 June 1997:A4). Another woman, Cleta Deatherage Mitchell, provided an interesting explanation:

> The distance between Washington and most of the American
> electorate . . . [is too far]. Most members of Congress can't
> commute daily and many can't commute weekly . . . [they are]
> like the non-custodial parent in a divorce family: they have
> visitations, they come on holidays and weekends, they send
> money . . . but they don't live with us. And over time it
> becomes harder and harder to really know one another very
> well. (Mitchell 1990)

Most politicians stay in Washington for as long as they can and gradually generate a "political class," as the archconservative George Will calls them (1997), a "culture of political professionalism," or of "career politicians," according to Petracca (1992b:41). They are members of what political scientists and sociologists like to label the "political power elite." Even opponents of term limits accept the explanations that lead to the development of these "entities" (Kesler, as cited in Benjamin and Malbin 1992:245-46; Fund, as cited in Benjamin and Malbin 1992:226-28; Kamber, Hyden, and Gephandt 1995:26). The disagreement whether the professionalism of the U.S. Congress and state legislatures (which began shortly after World War II) generated by the long stays in office has been a bad thing.

These different perceptions concerning the effects of term limits were also directly affected by developments that took place at the executive level: the imposition of the two-terms rule on the service of the president. Therefore, the essence of this disagreement would be addressed following the evolution of term limits idea at the executive level.

Term Limits at the Executive Level

The tyranny-phobia of Americans, whether due to populist sentiments of random majorities or the control of empowered minorities, seems to be more prevalent at the executive level than the congressional one. In Congress there are many participants, each with his or her set of preferences and interests. Therefore it is more difficult, but still possible, especially in times of national crisis, to reach tyrannical-type decisions. For example, during the Civil War, World War II, and even the Vietnam War, American governments conducted policies, often approved or ignored by Congress, toward parts of the population that were in direct contradiction to democratic values and norms.

However, the two levels of Congress, the electoral system, the party, and regional and state affiliations are among the factors that stand in the way of tyranny. It is less difficult, however, to find tyrants in the White House, and therefore limitation of presidential terms makes more sense.

Alexander Hamilton, a proponent of a strong central government and the principal opponent of term limits, was concerned, just like others, with tyrannical conduct. His remedy against such a possibility was that the elected would hold office for a considerable period, even a permanent one. This, he believed, would introduce "a principle of strength and stability in the organization of our government" (Malbin 1992:59). Just like David Hume, he rejected term limits because it would "operate as a constitutional interdiction of stability in the administration." It would also deprive the country of the "advantages of the experience gained by the chief magistrate in the exercise of his office." And finally, limiting the president's terms of office was "the banishing [of] men from station, in which, in certain emergencies of the state, their presence might be of the greatest moment to the public interest and safety" (Hamilton et al. 1991:103-104).

This last statement is interesting and deserves more attention. Hamilton, who together with Madison wrote the Federalist Papers, was no doubt a great thinker and a brilliant politician. In fact, his understanding of the theory and practice of politics and the way he was gradually able to maneuver the issues led to the construction of the Federal structure of government, protected by the Constitution. But his ideas for the new government, headed by a president who should serve for life, were so distant from what actually was included in the Constitution that it may lead some to wonder if he is entitled to his reputation. Certainly, it may even be somewhat perverse to find out that modern opponents of term limits use Hamilton's thoughts as a historical basis for rejecting this idea.

In the spirit of Riker's (1996) analysis of the politics of that era, we asked the following: Could it be that Hamilton made his radical points as a bargaining position against the anti-Federalists, knowing full well that his ideas would not be adopted? That is, was he willing to "lose" on some issues because the gains on others were more important? Choosing a president for life is indeed an anti-democratic concept, even for one who may admire the conducts of the British throne and its aristocracy. Justifying it on matters of emergency when great men and ruling experience are important is, at best, sheer demagogy. First, it may be that the president himself, because of his policy misconduct, is the one responsible for the "emergency" Second, the president does not operate alone. In situations of emergency, all capable men (and women, as in the case of Mrs. Woodrow Wilson, who effectively replaced her ailing husband during parts of his tenure), including past presidents, are recruited for the protection of the nation. Third, much of the problem that could be generated from cutting the term of the president short, even during times of grand national crises, is a result of the rigid Constitutional requirement to always hold election on the same designated day. Most parliamentary systems, especially the French and the British, two early models of democracies, are much more flexible on this matter. Indeed, often it seems that there, keeping elections on the designated date is the exception rather than the rule. Finally, using the extremes and the unique as a model for the normal and routine conducts of government is logically and practically wrong. Pointing to the danger that may evolve as a result of shortening the number of terms in office is merely a political manipulation. And Hamilton was good at that (Riker 1996).

The drafters of the Constitution did not accept Hamilton's position. They did not think that the president and the senate should be elected once, for life. They took the position that all those who hold elected posts, those who wish to continue to serve the public, should be required to obtain the approval of the voters each term. The decision of who would continue another term in office had thus been left for the voters to decide. In effect, however, all the American presidents until FDR chose to rule for only two terms. George Washington's voluntary departure from the presidency after his second term set the norm for presidential length of stay in office for almost one and a half centuries. Moreover, as Murry Rothband tells us, rotation (i.e., term limits) for everybody, elected politicians and appointees including bureaucrats, was effectively the case prior to the civil service reform beginning with the Pendleton Act in 1883 (as cited in Tabarrok 1994).

James Q. Wilson (1982:56) argues that the Founding Fathers had little to say about the nature and function of the executive branch of government and that the constitution is virtually silent on the subject. Indeed, "the debates in the Constitutional Convention are almost devoid of references to an administrative apparatus . . . there is no dispute in Congress that there should be executive departments, headed by single appointed officials. And, of course, the Constitution specified that these would be appointed by the President with the advice and consent of the Senate." Clearly, it was agreed or understood that the "President should have the sole right of removal . . . [that is to say] that the administrative system would wholly be subordinate—in law at least—to the president." It follows that when the president completed his service after two terms, so did the administration. The same practice, or guiding norm, holds for governors. They too were limiting their terms to only two, and consequently rotation in government became a widespread phenomenon. For years then, the idea of term limits did not surface and become a divisive political issue because it was actually practiced everywhere.

Consequently, the issue was not legally settled because it didn't need to be settled, and it did not, therefore, move to the center of public debate over the possible interpretations of the Constitution on this matter. But with Roosevelt's unprecedented four terms in office, the issue of limiting the amount of time the president may serve became a salient political issue and was settled, quite easily, by constitutional means.

The concerns of anti-Federalists and term limit supporters were settled when Washington set the tone for other public office holders by leaving after two terms. Executive tyranny, the greatest fear of people who lived under British rule, became a non-issue. That is, until the presidency of Andrew Jackson.

Jackson, a dedicated populist who prided himself on being a "common man," supported limiting terms of service to appointed office holders. He followed Jefferson, the most known proponent of term limits, who advocated limiting the amount of time an appointee may serve, on the grounds that it would help prevent the formation of a permanent bureaucracy. This indeed became a law with the passage of the "Tenure of Office Act" in 1820, limiting certain presidential appointees to a term of four years. But it was Jackson who saw the greatest display of the principle of rotation and term limits, where both the idea and the practice reached its apex and, ironically, "sowed the seed of its eventual demise" (Petracca 1992a:267).

In 1829, in his first annual message to Congress, Jackson declared that rotation among government employees was "a leading principle in the republican creed" (Cole 1993:40). He believed that the absence of limits of service on appointees made many of those officials corrupt and was counter to the principles of democracy. He also believed that the responsibilities of government officials were "so plain and simple" that any man of average intelligence could handle them, and that "no man has any more intrinsic right to official station than another" (Remini, 1981:190). Early in his presidency, Jackson wrote an "Outline of Principles" that instructed his cabinet officers to remove all those officials whose "moral habits" made them poor "examples of fidelity and honesty" (Cole 1993). Indeed, corruption was uncovered by this overhaul of the bureaucracy; almost $500,000 had been stolen from the Treasury Department (Remini 1981:191). This is a very big sum now, and for a period of little or no taxation, a much bigger sum. And, of course, the discovery provided a reconfirmation that his methods of handling government affairs were the right ones.

Despite this, Jackson's application of rotation had many critics, including some of the most prominent political figures of the time: Daniel Webster, John Calhoun, and Henry Clay. Others argued that his methods, in effect, politicized the bureaucracy, lowered the competence, violated the impartiality, and wrongly aggrandized the power of the executive branch—all in the name of rotation (Petracca 1992a:267). Indeed, that was, more or less, what he was doing. In the name of the term limits principle, especially as it applied to administrative officials, Jackson is most responsible for the initiation of the party patronage, better known as the "spoils system."

Before Jackson's presidency, the bureaucracy had grown greatly, from 3,000 employees at the turn of the century to nearly 12,000 people by 1830. Of the officials appointed directly by the president, Jackson removed almost half, a much higher ratio than any of his predecessors. Once the policy was established, this practice of removal flourished in future administrations and continues today. The percentage of removed officials grew under each succeeding president, reaching a high of 90 percent during Lincoln's tenure. A large number of removals occurred even when the party in power remained the same. Eventually, a demand for civil service reform emerged in the 1870s, after decades of removals by presidents eager to fill administrative officials with their own loyal people (Cole 1993:41). Promises of an attractive post in the federal government have thus become incentives for many to support a given presidential candidate.

Jackson believed he was upholding an inviolable democratic principle with his policy of removal. Removing government officials after a certain length of time would not only afford the opportunities for others to serve but would also reduce the possibilities for corruption. Of course, his formal or at least explicit intentions were that the competent, honest, and loyal would remain in office, and only those who were not capable or had not performed up to par with such normative requirements should be removed. It is difficult for taxpayers to argue against such a position.

Presented in this light, the principle of rotation was, thus, in good favor with both Congress and the American public. They accepted the right of the president to remove any of the personnel from previous administrations that seemed not to be fitted. They wanted the president to do so, to bring in good and capable people who were in agreement with his views of policy and governance. (Remini 1981:191). Not least important, congressmen felt no threat by such a policy; it was not their seats Jackson was looking to replace. But Jackson was a politician. Therefore, Jackson did not always base new appointments on merit; he often appointed to office, as most politicians do, friends and relatives. He was also fond of old soldiers, so he found jobs for them. Soon, government positions had turned into prizes, rewards for those who were loyal and did actual favors for the president. Consequently, cronyism, not competence and expertise, became the basis for many appointments and removals. All of this happened over many years, of course, right up to and during Lincoln's presidency. While it may not be historically fair to blame the effects of the patronage entirely on Jackson, his dedication to the principle of rotation in office helped produce some deleterious effects on the support for the issue.

The normative link between patronage and executive term limits is not difficult to trace. Both speak to a crucial issue in effective democracy: who should be in government and for how long. The arguments justifying patronage and term limits are similar. To help prevent corruption and isolation, democratic government requires that its appointed (or elected, if one wishes to extend the argument to the legislative branch) officials serve for only a short period. This allows the opportunity for people of many backgrounds and capabilities to participate in government service. In essence, this practice should keep government closer to the people and more responsive to their needs. Consequently, as the spoils system came under sharp attack during the last decades of the nineteenth century, support for term limits for both executive and legislative branches also declined. Because the reasons for this decline are so important for understanding the present developments of the legislative term limits issue, they will be further addressed in the next section.

In the meantime, the size of the administration grew enormously and, consequently, so grew the costs of covering expenses and the strength of that sector relative to the others.

Table 1.1   Civilian Employees of the Federal Government

Year	Paid Employees	Year	Paid Employees
1851	26,274	1918	854,000
1881	100,000	1940	1,042,420
1901	239,476	1945	3,816,310

Source: Palumbo, Dennis, and Steven Mayrard-Moody (1991).

Table 1.1 shows a gradual increase in the size of the government. The figures in this table refer only to civilian employees and not to the armed forces. It shows that every national crisis of major proportion (i.e., the Civil War, WWI, and WWII) brings more paid employees to the government in addition to the many military personnel. This means that following each election, politicians nominate more and more executives to positions in the federal government to manage the administration. Towering among the American presidents was Franklin Roosevelt, who was facing two of the greatest crises in American history during his administrations: the Great Depression and World War II. Indeed, during the years of the war against the Germans and the Japanese in both the European and the Pacific theaters, the size of the administration more than tripled.

Franklin Roosevelt's bid for a third presidential term in 1940 broke up the tradition of only two presidential terms. It forcefully brought the issue of executive term limits to the national attention. It reopened and intensified the debate that, while not settled, was far from becoming the central political issue of the day. His fourth successful bid for reelection, in 1944, and his death shortly thereafter, ignited constitutional steps to assure that such circumstances would not be reproduced. Consequently, the 22nd Amendment to the Constitution was passed in 1947, limiting the president to two four-year terms. This amendment was passed by the Republican-led 18th Congress and was ratified by the states in 1951. Nevertheless, the president still holds the right to remove and replace people in his administration.

President Roosevelt's decision to run for a third term was the direct result of the turmoil facing the United States in the 1930s and 1940s. But with the nation mired in the Great Depression and direct involvement in World War II becoming more and more likely, FDR decided to try to become the first president ever to be elected to three terms of office. His decision met with some opposition, even from members of his own party. For example, Democratic Senator Patrick McCarran said: "This is a government of law, and not of one man, however popular" (Goodwin 1994:107). The dominant political opinion in early 1940 was that, despite the crises the United States was facing and despite the president's enormous popularity, FDR should not seek reelection.

Roosevelt himself was apprehensive about breaking such an established presidential tradition; in a statement read at the Democratic Convention in July, 1940 he declared that he had "no wish to be a candidate again" (Goodwin 1994:125). The delegates, however, wanted nobody else but Roosevelt. In the end, the president's popularity and the perceived need for stable leadership in time of danger won out over the two-term tradition and the fear of executive tyranny. These conditions had not changed considerably by 1944; therefore, Roosevelt ran for a fourth time. He died soon after taking office, leaving the office to an inexperienced vice president who tackled the task of terminating the German and Japanese aggression against the free world.

Indeed, those days were the harshest in human history. Stability in government had been essential. In such times, the prime imperative of democracies is to protect themselves; all other political issues must be tabled. Elections are important, of course, but they reflect a "break," if not a crisis, in the inertia of the democratic public conduct. This may provide unnecessary advantages to the enemy. Great Britain, America's principle ally during the war, reacted to the external Nazi threat in a similar manner, even though their system of government is far different from the one practiced in their old colony. All members of Parliament tabled their political differences and together they formed a grand-coalition, which supported the prime minister, Winston Churchill, in his attempt to lead the country to victory. Here the Federalist's words of Hamilton, cited before, are most relevant because these were the times of "particular situations" when the nation required "an absolute necessity of the service of particular men," and that "their presence might be of the greatest moment of the public interest and safety." Indeed, FDR, the American, and Churchill, the British, (and, if one wants to be historically fair, Joseph Stalin the Soviet) were the leaders who rose to the challenge of history and saw their people to victory over the fascist oppressors in Europe and in the Pacific. Hamilton's words were heeded both by the delegates at the 1940 Democratic Convention and by a majority of the American people as well. Under the prevailing circumstances Roosevelt became the perfect public choice—indeed, the only choice.

When the threat to the existence of the political system is removed, divisive political issues can and usually do surface on the national agenda. The 18th Congress was not about to lose the opportunity to make a stand, and a negative one, on FDR's unprecedented election to four terms. The motivation of the new post-war Congress was, no doubt, largely political. The proposed amendment calling for a two-term restriction on presidents' tenures upset many. David McCullough, author of *Truman*, labeled it "a rebuke to the memory of Franklin Roosevelt and his four terms" (McCullough 1992:770). Contemporary Democrats, members of the 18th Congress, viewed the proposed amendment similarly. Even some Republicans openly admitted the anti-Roosevelt origins of the amendment, and debate on the Congress floor often centered on attacks and defenses of Roosevelt.

But there was also fear of tyranny, less intense, of course, than that expressed at the Constitutional Convention. The political and public concerns with the issue tell us a great deal about how highly Americans value placing restrictions on their leaders. It also tells us how fear of dictatorship, last endured in America during the colonial days of British rule, can still dictate public policy.

Executive and Legislature Professionalism

To complete the account of the evolution of the term limits debate, we first readdress the still-open question of the causes that led to the demise of the issue at the executive level when it was associated with the patronage system. Second, and in direct relationship to the debate that emerged during the 1990s of legislative term limits, we examine the essence of the criticism against the so-called and so often used term: the class of "professional legislators."

Regarding the first question, it would be a mistake to attribute the declining support for executive term limits on the mere corollary decline of the spoil system. There are other causes, more historical and sociological in origin, that played a significant role in the gradual erosion of support for term limits. We concentrate here on but one influential variable: the developments in the theory and practice of public administration.

Public administration is both an academic discipline and a professional enterprise. As a field of study, public administration emerged in the late nineteenth century. Until the mid-twentieth century, public administration was studied as a distinct field. Scholars attempted to isolate public administration from politics. After World War II, public administration was concerned with its relationship to the modern study of politics as a result of technological advancements, enhanced government responsibility, service provisions, and a closer analysis of the discipline. Is it a part of the political phenomenon, or should it be considered an independent area, detached on one hand but affected on the other by the influence of politics?

Interestingly, the man accredited with the distinguished title of the "father of the field" was the future president Woodrow Wilson. Wilson, a professor at Princeton and one of the few significant political scientists of that time who was neither trained abroad nor a European himself, wrote in 1887 a seminal essay entitled "The Study of Public Administration." There, impressed by the achievements of the new unified German bureaucracy, he looked for ways to emulate that successful model for the betterment of the management of public life in America. He argued that the new complexity in government, brought about by social and technological changes, required the development of an effective professional administrative machinery in government (Wilson 1887 in Stillman 1991:54). In essence, this meant that public administration should be independent of crass political machinations, especially the spoils system and patronage (Stillman 1991:54). The normative ideal behind the concept of separating politics and administration was to cleanse the administration of government from the muddy waters of the political processes. Eventually, the Progressive Party would use this idea of separation of politics and administration in its attempts to remove corruption from both.

Wilson was the first, but many followed suit. The first textbook of the new emerging academic field was written by Frank Goodnow in 1900. In that book, Goodnow calls for politicians to enact policies and administer public affairs impartially and nonpolitically. While naive in its approach, the organizing thesis has continued to be that well-trained professionals should manage the public domain, just as they do in the private sector. Indeed, Taylorism, the approach designed by Fredrich Taylor (1911), suggested a method of "Scientific Management" for both public and private sectors. Responding to the new developments in industrial methodology of mass production and in the size and functions of government, Taylor specified how to obtain efficiency (i.e., through the "time and motion" studies) in operation. Hence, training programs were established at many universities where scholars made the study of public administration their area of research. Indeed, in the early part of the century, many of these scholars believed, as some still do, that it is possible to separate politics from administration and therefore possible to manage public affairs in accordance with some set of well-established criteria—in effect, scientific principles. The two scholars most recognized for this approach were Gulick and Urwick (1937). Gulick (1987), for example, specified criteria like "planning," "staffing," "directing," or "coordinating" as principles that should guide the administrators. Some years earlier, in 1916, the French practitioner Henry Fayol (1987) had written on the "General Principles of Management," especially organizational hierarchy and "unity of command." Followed by Chester Barnard (1938), both proposed a more realistic, less self-contradictory approach to management. While the

Scientific Management orientation was not a passing fad, especially in the private sector where efficiency is a highly valued criterion, the "scientific merits" of the "findings" of the "scientists" of public administration came under growing criticism. Herbert Simon, for example, launched a bold attack in the early 1940s on the entire approach, which likened these "findings" to "proverbs" (1987); that is, each administrative problem could be explained by a proverb but also by one that means quite the opposite. Instead, he and his followers offered a scientifically grounded theory of administrative behavior (Simon 1967; Cyert and March 1963; March and Simon 1987).

But the sincere attempts to introduce rationality into the work of the administration, long-term planning, costs/benefits analysis, coupled with knowledge accumulated in other "legitimate" scientific disciplines, like economics or psychology, continued. They guided government activities in, for example, the area of social planning (Colleman 1966) or in the management of the national and state budgets (Berkley 1978). And while the insensitivity to the presence of political and other variables led to failures of public programs in these areas (Wildavsky 1974), no one today would seriously challenge the concept that the public domain should be managed by educated, well-trained professionals. To use an extreme example: no one would propose that modern warfare would be fought by an army (which is indeed an important part of the public bureaucracy) of untrained citizens, however highly motivated. Appleby (1949) was among the first to challenge the set of beliefs that defines private administrators as somewhat "better" than their public counterparts. He asked, for example, who is subject to more pressures and privileges? In the comparison that he offered, the public officials did not fare well.

The work of government in modern society is complex and demanding. It needs people who will dedicate their time to acquire the skills, experience, and expertise to do just as Max Weber (1958) recommended. To limit their terms in office would mean cutting off the legs on which modern polities stand. This, however, has nothing to do, at least not directly, with limiting the terms of the president. The person filling this post has several hats; among them the principal one, which attracted the support of the people in the first place, is the political one—his vision for the country. He need not be a great administrator, although he is the head of the executive branch. He need not be a courageous warrior, although he is the commander-in-chief. He need not be an experienced diplomat, although he represents the country in the international community. He just has to know how to make decisions consistent with his vision. Or, as Andrew Jackson said: to have common sense.

The president may rely for that matter on "his team," as Gerald Ford, a Republican vice president who turned president, justified the removal of many of President Richard Nixon's Republican loyalists after assuming office in 1974. These new loyalists were trusted by Ford and could help him meet his vision. They could therefore replace the members who were brought in by the old administration, most of whom were Republican too. They, in turn, like the ones replaced by them, had to rely on the permanent system of experienced professional bureaucrats.

At the top, then, where decisions over policy directions are made, the American model of the executive branch is not much different from bureaucracies guided and staffed by party ideologues in other countries, where all are committed to a certain political way. Below that level, the American system is closer to the British model of civil service. This model has been internalized by most Americans, and because it has worked for so long and seems to be an integrated part of the political culture, it attracts few, if any, criticisms.

Legislative term limits are a different matter. They are often confused with executive term limits because proponents and opponents used identical concepts, such as "professionalism" or "careerism," to describe their preferences over these issues. For example, in an essay entitled "Congressional Terms Limits: A Bad Idea Whose Time Should Never Come," Thomas Mann sets out to defend what is often pejoratively referred to as "legislative careerism" (1994). To Mann, the support of term limits means ultimately the rejection of professionalism and careerism in politics. He raises serious and fundamental questions about such loosely tossed-around words. He points out the confusion of the supposed evils of careerism that term limits supporters hope to remedy. Indeed, some supporters, including George Will, argued that careerism produces legislators who are virtual slaves to the public whim, unwilling and incapable of exercising independent judgment (Will 1991). To Mann and to many political scientists, far from being an evil, increased careerism and professionalism is a "necessary offshoot of the growth and specialization of the modern world" (Mann 1994:87). Decreasing or eliminating professionalism is, then, neither possible nor desirable: a Hume- or Hamiltonian-type argument adjusted to modern times.

If one spuriously takes such an argument into consideration, then one cannot escape the implications that elected representatives should be highly educated and specialized in the complexities of modernization. They should be scientists, engineers, or at least lawyers, well versed and experienced in the small scriptures of public law. These are professions of which most people have little knowledge; hence it is difficult to determine who really masters his or her field and who just pretends to do so. One would certainly prefer that the representatives' record of expertise would be presented to the public before they stand for election, and one would oppose their learning on the job with taxpayers' money. The fact is, however, that politicians are elected not because of their professional skills but because of other attributes believed to be important for representing those who vote for them, or because voters simply dislike the opposing candidate. Nowhere in democracies are there schools training young boys and girls to become presidents, senators, or just "simple" representatives. However, experience in governmental posts may not be detrimental for one who seeks an elected position.

Mann is promoting the concept that politicians should be "better than" the people they represent, as opposed to the alternative guiding concept of representative government that they should be "like" the people they represent. But, no doubt, those experienced politicians are different from most people anyway, because they stand for election and reelection over and over again, creating the so-called "political class." The members of this class are willing to do things most people are not. They sacrifice their time, money, family life, and often their ego and pride in order to secure their political positions. Non-stop politicking becomes a way of life for many, and they are willing to do much, very much, to keep it that way. Their sacrifices fall short of giving up their political position, of course. In chapter 3 the conditions that are conducive for the creation of this real or perceived class will be analyzed. For now, it is left to ask what type of skills a representative really needs to effectively manage public affairs.

Legal background never hurts, and therefore the proportion of lawyers in most modern parliaments is high compared to representatives of other professions. Indeed, where the law governs, as is the case in the United States, there should be people who can write and read the law. But in the last three decades, the proportion of lawyers serving in Congress has considerably decreased. In 1969, 58 percent of the Congress were lawyers. The number has dropped to only 42 percent in 1999. On the state level, the proportion cascaded during that period even more dramatically (Perez-Pena 1999). But legal knowledge is not the most important attribute. David Hume, John Adams, and many others flushed out the prime political attribute that should be expected from a representative: common sense. This is not gained by more experience or a longer stay. What politicians gain in the Congress over time is the knowledge of how to make deals, how to bargain (Doron and Sened 2001), how to trade votes (Riker and Brams 1973), how to manipulate the agenda (Riker 1986), and how to become champions of very specific issues (Wildavsky 1974), sometimes relating to interests that are foreign to most of their voters (Fenno 1978). This may be a result of the complexity of modern life, but no one, not even the most experienced politician, has a comprehensive understanding of all these matters.

It is thus somewhat shortsighted to bring defenses against legislative term limits on grounds of the "specific skills" required from modern politicians, skills that are, however, not required of the president, whose terms are limited to two. If they do not know the ropes and web of government, then they should get the proper professional help, as presidents do. The issue should thus be addressed, not in terms of efficiency in government but in terms of the principles that should guide free societies and free people.

Chapter Two

The Constitutional Legal Barrier:
U.S. Term Limits, Inc. v. Thornton

There will come a revolt of the people
against the capitalists, unless the aspiration of the people
is given some adequate legal expression.
—Louis Brandeis, 1933

The idea of legislative term limits resurfaced in 1990 in the form of restrictions that were adopted by three states. It was the product of the activities of grassroots movements and proponents of the issue. Their members expressed disappointment with the conduct and quality of the political system. Because only a constitutional amendment can limit the terms of U.S. senators and representatives and because constitutional amendments are so difficult to enact, the term limits movement adopted a bypassing strategy. In each of the designated states, they proposed practical restrictions, not legal prohibitions that are unconstitutional, to be imposed on incumbents seeking additional terms.

This practice, which became popular and was soon adopted in other states, raised several important questions; most important among them concerns the relationships between the federal and state authorities. Other questions brought the issue right back to the old debate that took place between the Federalists and the anti-Federalists. In 1995, the Supreme Court was asked to rule on the issue. It reaffirmed the original

Federalist position for not including term limits, or restrictions that in effect limit terms of U.S. congressmen, into the Constitution.

This chapter reviews the background for that Court decision. Then, the opinion of the majority is presented, followed by the opinion of the minority. We then concentrate our attention on two points that were made by the majority: the intentions of the Framers and the "people's right to be elected" as a different concept from the one commonly used, namely "the people's right to choose." Finally, by way of concluding remarks, we provide an overall assessment of this important court ruling.

The 1995 Supreme Court Decision: Background

Certainly the most important legal case to emerge from the term limits movement is *U.S. Term Limits, Inc., et al. v. Thornton et al.* (1995). It originated in Arkansas, rose up the judicial chain of command in that state from trial court to the state supreme court, and eventually was heard by the United States Supreme Court. In a five to four vote, the U.S. Supreme Court made one of its most important recent decisions, one that has had and presumably will continue to have a profound impact on the term limits movement, its strategies, political clout, and its effects on public policy.

In 1992, voters in Arkansas approved an amendment to the state constitution that banned from the general election ballot any candidate who had already served three terms in the U.S. House of Representatives or two terms in the U.S. Senate. The amendment did not therefore impact "term limits," at least not in the strict sense that a candidate was prohibited from serving in office after a certain number of terms. The imposition was a ballot access restriction, which does not preclude an incumbent from seeking reelection as often as he or she likes, but only prohibits his or her name from appearing on the ballot. Note that there were no restrictions on write-in candidacies.

The supposed distinction between ballot access restriction and fixed term limit laws is worth discussing because Amendment 73 to the Arkansas Constitution attempted to make use of it. State office holders such as the governor, attorney general, and state representatives and senators were all given direct, fixed term limits: incumbents were prohibited from serving in office if they had already served a certain number of terms. By treating state and federal office holders differently, one could claim, as Victor Kamber did, that the amendment's draftees were not adhering to any principles of democracy and representation, but were merely making a crass political attempt to make Amendment 73 more constitutionally palatable (Kamber, Hyde, and Gephardt 1995). The question of whether a ballot access restriction does in fact constitute an outright prohibition was one of several issues the Supreme Court attempted to resolve in its 1995 decision.

Amendment 73 became a legal issue almost immediately after it was approved. Just ten days after the vote, Bobbie Hill, acting on behalf of herself, the League of Women Voters in Arkansas, and, in her words, "citizens, residents, taxpayers, and registered voters" of Arkansas, filed a complaint in an Arkansas circuit court, claiming that Amendment 73 was "unconstitutional and void." Ms. Hill claimed that qualifications for members of the U.S. Congress were specifically delineated in the U.S. Constitution and could not be altered by the states. U.S. Term Limits, Inc., which had joined forces with Arkansas officials, countered by arguing that the tenth amendment to the U.S. Constitution gives the states broad authority to regulate elections. Furthermore, the constitutional provision giving states the authority to regulate the time, place, and manner of elections also provides for ballot access restrictions on incumbents. The Court agreed with Ms. Hill, charging that the amendment violated Article I of the U.S. Constitution, (*U.S. Term Limits, Inc. v. Hill*, 316 Ark. 251 [1994]).

In a five-to-two vote, the Arkansas Supreme Court affirmed the decision of the circuit court. Justice Robert L. Brown, writing for the majority, spoke of the need for "uniformity" of representation in the Congress. He concluded that individual states have no authority "to change, add to, or diminish" the requirements for congressional service set forth in the U.S. Constitution.

The Arkansas Supreme Court also refused to make the distinction between ballot access restrictions and strict term limits. Concluding that the practical effects of a ballot access restriction are the same as the effects of strict term limits, Justice Brown wrote that any "glimmers of opportunity . . . are faint indeed—so faint in our judgment, that they cannot salvage Amendment 73 from constitutional attack." In a dissenting opinion, Chief Justice Cracraft did argue that a ballot access restriction was completely different in nature from a strict term limits law. The difference was one between a rule that "imposes an absolute bar on incumbent succession" and one that "merely makes it more difficult for an incumbent to be elected" (*U.S. Term Limits, Inc. v. Hill*, 316 Ark. 251 [1994]). After the ruling, the state of Arkansas and U.S. Term Limits, Inc. petitioned for a writ of certiorari, and the Supreme Court obliged.

Before turning to the presentation of the majority opinion, an important point needs to be examined concerning the Arkansas court's reasoning. Indeed, it may be argued that restrictions on ballot access are, in effect, term limits. This practice is common in many democratic systems where citizens, voters as well as candidates, are excluded from the electoral process due to technicalities and not by legal prohibitions. For example, registration requirements may become in some places an effective obstacle to voting, especially for people with limited language knowledge. While qualifications for representatives are spelled out in the Constitution, in 1990 over 95 percent of the incumbents who asked to be reelected returned to U.S. Congress. This is, in effect, but in no way illegal, a circumvention of the principles of "fairness" and "free election," a frustrating practical situation sought to be solved by the term limits movement, by practical means. The court in Arkansas and, as we shall see, the U.S. Supreme Court, did not address the important question concerning the actual practice that restricts the people's right to be elected, which is less damaging to democracy. The last section of this chapter provides some partial answers to this question.

The Majority Opinion

Justice John Paul Stevens wrote the U.S. Supreme Court majority opinion. At the beginning of the sixty-one page opinion, Justice Stevens recognized two issues for the court to resolve: whether the U.S. Constitution forbids the states from altering in any way the qualifications for congressional membership enumerated in the Constitution, and whether the distinction between a ballot access restriction and a strict term limits law was of any constitutional significance (*U.S. Term Limits, Inc., et al. v. Thornton et al.*, 1995). In the following paragraphs, citations are presented from this Supreme Court ruling.

By the slimmest majority, a five to four vote, the Supreme Court affirmed the decisions of the Arkansas Supreme and circuit courts. The majority opinion was a thoroughly argued piece, covering in detail relevant precedents, the Framers' intent, and an examination of the wording of the Constitution. The majority also attempted to resolve the more fundamental issues of federalism and the question of sovereignty in a Federalist government.

The controlling precedent in the majority's case was *Powell v. McCormack* (395 U.S. 486, 1966). In that case, the controversial representative Adam Clayton Powell had been reelected to his position as a member of the House of Representatives. Investigations made into his misconduct led a select house committee to determine his eligibility to take the representative position. The committee found that although Powell met the age, residency, and citizenship requirements, his financial misconduct warranted exclusion from membership. Powell filed suit, claiming that excluding him on that basis was unconstitutional because Art. I, Sec. 2 of the Constitution set exclusive qualifications for House membership. The Supreme Court agreed with Powell, maintaining that the Congress "has no authority to exclude any person, duly elected by his constituents, who meets all the requirements for membership expressly prescribed in the Constitution." (395 U.S. 521, 522). In relying on this case, Stevens argued that Powell stood for the proposition "that the people should choose whom they please to govern them."

As was the case with *Powell, Thornton* spoke directly to the issue of whether constitutionally outlined qualifications for membership to the U.S. Congress could be altered. Once again, the Court ruled that Congress could not alter the Constitution's specifically delineated requirements.

To argue this, Stevens also invoked James Madison and the Framers in justifying the majority decision. Federalist No. 52 and Federalist No. 57, according to Stevens and the majority, offer "affirmative evidence" that the Framers intended for the states to "have no role in the setting of qualifications" for U.S. congressional legislators. According to the majority, one of the Framers' primary concerns regarding federal elections was the prevention of undue state interference. Quoted at great length in the majority's decision are several passages in Federalist No. 52 and Federalist No. 57, both authored by Madison, which speak directly to the issue of qualifications for elected federal officials.

Invoking the authority of the Framers is meaningless if the Constitution itself is not looked at to determine the constitutionality of a law. The majority contended that the fear of the abuse of state power in federal elections, spoken of at various points in the Federalist Papers, is reflected in the Constitution in certain "provisions" intended to minimize the possibility of state interference in federal elections. For example, to prevent discrimination against federal electors, the Framers required in Art. I, Sec. 2, cl.1, that "the qualifications for federal electors be the same as those for state electors." Also, despite having the constitutional authority to regulate the "Times, Places and Manner" of elections, the states' power is again held in check by the Constitution through the reserved right of Congress to "make or alter such regulations." All this leads the majority to the conclusion that "the specification of fixed qualifications in the constitutional text was intended to prescribe uniform rules that would preclude modification by either Congress or the States."

The Constitution declares in Art. I, Sec. 5, that "Each House shall be the Judge of the Elections, Returns, and Qualifications of its own Members." According to the majority, this is further evidence that qualifications for federal legislators are fixed and that only the federal government has the authority to rule on a federal legislator's qualifications. Stevens writes, "If the States had the right to prescribe additional qualifications . . . state law would provide the standard for judging a Member's eligibility."

The majority also found the absence of any provision for term limits in the Constitution "compelling." As Stevens correctly indicates, the issue of term limits was a "major source of controversy." Opponents of ratification decried the lack of a term limits provision in the Constitution; some proponents of ratification were also concerned with this. Several amendments were proposed during ratification that would have required term limits. Stevens again invokes the Federalists, arguing that their "responses to those criticisms and proposals addressed the merits of the issue, arguing that rotation was incompatible with the people's right to choose." The incompatibility with the "people's right to choose" was an important argument of the Federalists during ratification, and an important argument of the Supreme Court's during the *Powell* and *Thornton* cases.

What is more to the point, according to Stevens and the majority, is not which side has the better argument in the term limits debate, but rather if the states can require term limits for federal legislators. Stevens writes:

> Regardless of which side has the better of the debate over rotation, it is most striking that nowhere in the extensive ratification debates have we found any statement by either a proponent or opponent of rotation that the draft constitution would permit States to require rotation for the representatives of their own citizens. If the participants in the debate had believed that States retained the authority to impose term limits, it is inconceivable that the Federalists would not have made this obvious response to the arguments of the pro-rotation forces. The absence in an otherwise freewheeling debate of any suggestion that States had the power to impose additional qualifications unquestionably reflects the Framers' common understanding that States lacked that power.

The majority believed, therefore, that there is no "assumption" that the states could add qualifications for federal legislators. If there were such an assumption, it would have been a sound response to the arguments the Federalists advanced. Not only did the majority use the Constitution and the history of its drafting as an authority to guide its decision, but it also used congressional experience and what it calls "fundamental principles of representative democracy."

In 1807, Representative William McCreery of Maryland was initially prevented from taking his seat because of a residency requirement imposed by that state (Benjamin and Malbin 1992:256). A report of the House Committee on Elections determined that qualifications of House members were unalterably enumerated by the Constitution, and the full House voted to reinstate McCreery. This ruling was instrumental in the Court's decision in the Powell case, and the House's vote on McCreery's eligibility has long been held as a vindication of the view that the states cannot add to the qualifications of members established in the Constitution.

The Senate has also had similar experiences. In 1887, Senator Charles Faulkner of West Virginia was ruled ineligible to serve by that state because of a provision in its constitution. But the Senate Committee on Privileges and Elections ruled that "no state can prescribe any qualification to the office of United States Senator in addition to those declared in the United States Constitution." (quoted in Benjamin and Malbin).

Therefore, according to the majority, precedence, the Constitution, the debate at the founding, and the subsequent congressional practice, qualifications for federal legislators are fixed, and no state can add to what the Constitution exhaustively delineates. But the majority was not satisfied with relying on the above authorities for their decision. It takes a philosophical approach in its reliance on "democratic principles" to further bolster its argument that states cannot impose term limits on congressional members.

According to the majority, the right of the people to "choose whom they please to govern them" is recognition of an egalitarian ideal, an ideal that was critical in the construction of the Constitution. This ideal, writes Stevens, was recognized by the Framers throughout the debates over ratification and further supported by the Supreme Court in the *Powell* decision. In Federalist No. 57 Madison wrote: "Who are to be the objects of popular choice? Every citizen whose merit may recommend him to the esteem and confidence of his country." The majority also quotes several others who, during the debate over ratification, spoke of the right of every man to run for public office as long as he has the confidence of the people.

The last principle the majority invoked is the idea that "the right to choose representatives belongs not to the states but to the people." This, according to the majority, is crucial to the entire idea of a federal government and the principle of federalism. Justice Paul Stevens writes:

> From the start, the Framers recognized that the "great and radical vice" of the Articles of Confederation was "the principle of legislation for states or governments, in their corporate or collective capacities and as contradistinguished from the individuals of whom they consist," The Federalist No. 15, at 108 (Hamilton). Thus the Framers, in perhaps their most important contribution, conceived of a federal government directly, not by States, but by the people. The Framers implemented this ideal most clearly in the provision, extant from the beginning of the republic, that calls for Members of the House of Representatives to be "chosen every second Year by the People of the several States." Art. I, Sec. 2, cl. 1. Following the adoption of the 17th Amendment in 1913, this ideal was extended to elections for the Senate. The Congress of the United States, therefore, is not a confederation of nations in which separate sovereigns are represented by appointed delegates, but is instead a body composed of representatives of the people (U.S. Term Limits, Inc. v. Thornton, 29).

The majority maintains that it is the right of the people, not the right of the states, to choose representatives. This controversy over sovereignty, the question of whether it is the nation as a whole or the individual states that have the right to choose the nation's elected officials, lies at the very core of federalism and republican government. It brings back the sounds of the past, when the Federalists, headed by Hamilton, debated the anti-Federalists over the shapes, the design, and the institutions of the new republic. States passing term limit legislation for federal officials brings the issue of sovereignty again to the forefront, where it can be resolved only by the courts or by a long and difficult process of amending the Constitution.

Finally, the majority examines whether Arkansas' Amendment 73 can be considered a "qualification" since it is not a strict term limits law but only a ballot access restriction, and thus could be considered a permissible exercise of state power to regulate the "Times, Places, and Manners of Holding Elections." The majority rejects that view, using much the same argument as the Arkansas Supreme Court did when it too rejected that distinction. Stevens writes: "In our view, Amendment 73 is an indirect attempt to accomplish what the Constitution prohibits Arkansas from accomplishing directly." The Arkansas Supreme Court described the ballot access restriction as an "effort to dress eligibility to stand for Congress in ballot access clothing" (316 Ark, 266). The majority of the U.S. Supreme Court agreed. Examining the intent and effect of Amendment 73, Stevens argues that it is impossible to believe that the intent of the amendment is anything other than an attempt "to prevent the election of incumbents" and an "attempt to achieve a result that is forbidden by the Federal Constitution." Thus, no meaningful distinction can be made between strict term limits legislation and ballot access restrictions since the intended effect of each is the same.

The Minority Opinion

The minority opinion, written by Justice Clarence Thomas, contends that "Nothing in the Constitution deprives the people of each State of the power to prescribe eligibility requirements for the candidates who seek to represent them in Congress. The Constitution is simply silent on this question. And where the Constitution is silent, it raises no bar to action by the States or the people." According to the minority, the majority's decision is based on a fundamental misunderstanding of the notion of "reserved powers." Thomas argues that there need not be any specific provision in the Constitution that grants the states the right to create qualifications for their representatives in Congress.

Essentially, the minority opinion in *U.S. Term Limits, Inc., et al. v. Thornton et al.* bases its entire argument on one paragraph written by Justice Thomas, one that speaks to the very heart of the Federalist controversy that prevailed in the United States.

Our system of government rests on one overriding principle: all power stems from the consent of the people. To phrase the principle in this way, however, is to be imprecise about something important to the notion of "reserved" powers. The ultimate source of the Constitution's authority is the consent of the people of each individual state, not the consent of the undifferentiated people of the nation as a whole.

According to Thomas, the principle that governs this issue is found in the 10th Amendment, which declares that all powers not delegated to the federal government nor prohibited to the states are reserved to the states. Thomas contends that where the Constitution does not either "expressly or by necessary implication" prohibit the states from employing a particular power or privilege, then the states enjoy it.

The minority's argument in this case rests on a broad interpretation of "states' rights." In fact, the entire disagreement between the majority and minority in this case can be traced to a disagreement over the principles of federalism and the power of the federal government as it relates to the powers of the individual states.

Justice Anthony Kennedy, in a concurring opinion, contends that the minority opinion in *Thornton* "runs counter to fundamental principles of federalism." According to Kennedy, citizens in the United States have two distinct political capacities: they are both citizens of the United States and citizens of their individual state of residence. Because of this duality in citizenship, each sphere of government is to be controlled without interference from the other. Kennedy writes: "the federal character of congressional elections flows from the political reality that our National Government is republican in form and that national citizenship has privileges and immunities protected from state abridgment by the force of the Constitution itself." This means that Arkansas or any other state may not interfere with the relationship between the national government and those expressing a federal right of citizenship. To do so, according to Kennedy, would violate the duality of our federalism.

Justice Kennedy's picture of two separated political entities is conceptually interesting. It seems, however, to be a somewhat creative interpretation of the Constitution. In fact, the Constitution itself provides the mechanism of amendments by which states can ignite a process that would, if completed, affect the boundaries of the federal entity. The protection the federal entity has against the potential ambition of the states to curve its identity boundaries and sovereignty is the Constitutional requirement to obtain special majorities on the state and congressional levels in order to confirm an amendment. This status quo-oriented requirement sets a very real and effective political obstacle on states' intentions. The court simply ordered to sustain the status quo.

Term limits supporters did not like the ruling of the Supreme Court, to say the least. Paul Jacob, U.S. Term Limits executive director, referred to this decision in the following words: "It is not fair that the country's most powerful judges are paying back their friends in the Congress for giving them the only job that offers lifelong job security!" (cited in Detweiler 1996). Indeed, the Supreme Court's decision, as divisive and controversial as it was, did ultimately settle the question of whether the individual states could impose term limits on federal lawmakers. By answering this question negatively, the Supreme Court could not banish the term limits movement in the United States, but it has inadvertently caused it to almost completely alter its strategy.

The term limits movement has essentially conceded defeat in this area and has instead concentrated its efforts on enacting term limits for legislators on the state level. Also, in an attempt to influence Congress on this issue, the term limits movement, led by such groups as U.S. Term Limits, has sought to prevail upon congressional members and candidates to take a stand on the issue of term limits for federal legislators. They thus offered pledges for members of Congress to sign a promise to leave office voluntarily after a fixed number of terms. Ultimately, however, the Supreme Court's decision in the *Thornton* case had such a great impact that it is possible, and perhaps even useful, to speak of the recent history of the term limits movement as being divided into two phases: pre-*Thornton* and post-*Thornton*.

People's Right to be Elected

There is a great political beauty in the ruling of the Supreme Court. It is as if the judges played the role of Rabbinical scholars, using the Constitution like a biblical source of epistemological authority, and the Federalist Papers like they were its Talmudic source for interpretations. But things have changed since the early days of the nation. The federal government is safe, secured, and sound, and no one, not even members of the great state of Texas or, for that matter, Michigan (see chapter 6), is threatening to alter this situation. There are two different dimensions in the Court decision: the legality of the Arkansas Access Restriction and the interpretation of the Framers' intent, in light of the developments occurring since the drafting of the Constitution.

The first dimension causes no problem. Indeed, limitations imposed on access are identical to legal restrictions. And if the latter is prohibited by the Constitution, so must be the former. If people wish to change this matter, they are free to amend the Constitution. This is the American way, a way that has induced stability in government. So the question here is not right or wrong from a normative point of view but from a legal one.

The second dimension is problematic indeed. It involves interpretation of the essence of American citizenship, the nature of the qualifications needed for representatives of both federal and state governments, the nature of the relations between both of these governments, and the meaning of what the majority of judges called the "Principles of Democracy." In this respect, Justice Kennedy's position mentioned above is most important. Hence, we return to the brief comment made before regarding his interpretation of the constitution.

He distinguishes between two levels of citizenry: state and national. The second level is not only sovereign over the first, but it should not even be affected by it. To simplify, what is meant by this notion is that the states are merely serving as unequal and differently weighted voting zones to select members to the Congress. The weights are determined by the size of their population. This may indeed reflect present reality, but it is difficult to be convinced that the anti-Federalists would accept it without launching a major political fight. The fact is that after more than 200 years of functioning federal and state governments (including during the Civil War, which could easily be perceived as a war over the correct interpretation of the Constitution), much of the "sovereignty" and independence of the states has been eroded. Nonetheless, since representatives are sent to the Senate by people who wish them to represent their specific needs at home, it is conceivable that they would also expect that those sent would be selected with their senders' wishes in mind. Unlike regular voting zones, whose borders are often designed on geographic basis or in accordance with the size of the population (as is the case within the states), representatives to the Senate are selected from historically determined political entities.

One could easily think of methods to avoid confusion in determining boundaries between two political entities to make sure that their political mechanisms (e.g., voting systems) overlap as little as possible. For example, popular election of the president could be decided not through the intermediate institution of the Electoral College, and representatives could be selected not in accordance with the existing district design but with, say, a regional design (west, north, south, east, etc.). Although unrealistic and used just to make the point, such differentiating designs may produce a desired separating effect. The Framers could have selected any type of design to emphasize the differences between the two entities. The design that was chosen and is explicitly defined in the Constitution is merely a reflection of the interests and the power relationship that existed at that time between the Federalists and the anti-Federalists. The Court, the guardian of the Constitution, reconfirms in its ruling the resolution arrived at during the early days of the republic.

But the hierarchical relationship between the two levels of governments as prescribed by the Constitution and intended by the Framers seems to require "uniformity" in the rules and, as the majority of judges demanded, also in "qualifications for federal electors [to] be the same as those for state electors." This may be a just requirement in principle but it is very difficult to attain in practice. Uniformity is obtained merely in one place: in the list of candidates' names that appear on the ballots. Once these names are placed on the ballots, the act of voting has been similar across the states, and so are the methods used to tabulate those votes to determine winners and losers. However, the political forces in the different states use different methods to select and name their candidates. Primaries, caucuses, write-in endorsements, or conventions are some of these methods. Hence, the principle political question, not the legal one, should not just relate to voters' "freedom of choice" (an issue to be discussed from a theoretical perspective in the next chapter) or who has the right to be elected, but who has the chance to be elected.

A right grounded in the Constitution is one thing; a material or practical chance to obtain it is another. The rights of minorities and of women as citizens are secured by the Constitution, but without the liberal interpretations of the Court in the early sixties and government's enacting on that basis, African American representations would have materialized at an even slower pace. There are several practical, not legal, barriers that reduce the chances of many Americans from being elected; a right specified in the Constitution but which is not secured in reality. Prime among them is the advantages incumbents have over their challengers, an advantage that prevents many from having a fair chance of being elected. A functioning democracy, one that was certainly envisioned by the Framers, should attempt to remove the unfair political advantages some citizens have over others. The Court seemed to ignore the developments that occurred over the years, especially after World War II, whereby congressmen made their political service a lifetime occupation, blocking the way of others from serving. The Court in its ruling correctly referred to the "Principles of Democracy"; however, a fair chance of being elected is indeed such an important principle.

It is against the power of the incumbency and its adverse effects on the quality of the democratic life in America that the people of the states were protesting. The Court's decision is important in reinstating the symbolic value of federal supremacy over the states. It did not, however, help in providing a remedy for the ill-functioning sources of unreflective representation. It thus made people divert their energy from the federal to the state level. But it kept the issue of legislative term limits on the public agenda, to be continually addressed on all levels.

Conclusion

Constitutions, like any sets of laws, are a formal reflection of compromises, solutions to potential or actual conflicts between different interests. Robert North writes (1968:230): "The functioning of a given law is usually to prevent conflict, to resolve conflict, or to constrain conflict within agreed upon limits." The American Constitution reflects, among other things, an equilibrium that was obtained with great difficulty between the opposing interests of the Federalists and the anti-Federalists in the days of the nation's formation. It was a compromise made over the issue and the nature of federal and states' sovereignty. The 1995 Supreme Court decision upheld the status quo. By holding a state-initiated law unconstitutional, the Court ruled that it is not a side to the renewed debate. This means that the said conflict should be settled by other methods that are provided by the Constitution. It has been one and a half centuries since the Supreme Court ruled a state law unconstitutional. The Court's response was the 13th Amendment, which prohibited slavery (Rotunda 1995). Regarding term limits, the ruling has redirected much of the supporters' energy.

The Supreme Court ruling can be overturned only by a constitutional amendment. Because Congress is unlikely to approve one, the initiative must come from the states. Twenty-two states have enforced one or another kind of term limitation on their elected representatives. Assuming that this group of states will continue to uphold its positions, twelve more states are needed to call for a convention to draft an amendment. This task is difficult indeed. The process may take a long time. Constitutional Convention ("Con-Con") is an instrument that has not been tried yet. While the drive in the various states to convince legislators to approve such a Con-Con continues with varied intensity, it is unlikely that it will ever be materialized. Something else, however, might work.

Voters who support term limits must internalize the idea that they should not vote in favor of candidates who serve more than two or three terms. A long process of socialization can attain this. Socialization occurs through constant exposure to an issue. Keeping term limits high on the political agenda by public exposure of the issue through the spoken and printed media may partly create this effect. Likewise, reminding the voters by various methods (e.g., written commitments as in Colorado, or notations on the ballots that inform the voters that certain representatives "disregard" or "decline" to support term limits) that their choice of representative is for or against term limitation may contribute to this long-term effect. If successful, such a goal-oriented social drive may establish a norm, which would be very difficult for the Congress (and for that matter the Court) to ignore.

The story with the 17th Amendment shows that this route, which is long and demands a lot of patience, could be effective (Bandow 1996). The first move for an amendment of a popular election of U.S. senators was proposed in Congress in 1826. Because it stood against the very self-interest of the senators, who were chosen by state legislators, it was tabled without discussion. But because public sentiments over this issue were broad, opponents found it more and more difficult to block the reform. In 1893, 1894, and in 1898, the House approved the amendment but the Senate refused to support it. Toward the end of the 19th century, the idea that senators should be elected like House representatives was so implanted in the minds of the voters that their preferences were shaped accordingly. They made their preferences known through primaries. By 1901, Oregon's voters forced their state legislators to commit themselves to the voters' choice of senators to be selected by an advisory election. By 1904, the people of Oregon, by use of the initiative, passed a state law that allowed a virtual direct election of their senators, so that the choice of senators became, in effect, the privilege of the people and nobody else. Other states followed suit, and soon the practice became a norm. The norm became most salient in the southern states, whose politics was, in effect, controlled by the Democratic party. There, voters chose their Senate candidates in a special primary election; the state legislators just approved the people's choices.

Consequently, the states began submitting applications for the calling of a Con-Con. This indeed constituted a real threat to the congressmen who did not wish to place themselves against the people, their voters. Soon after, the Congress, including the Senate, adopted the amendment that became part of the Constitution. By 1912, the people in twenty-nine of the forty-eight states were already picking senators directly. The 17th Amendment was approved in that year without much effective opposition. Following such a long-term strategy may very well work for term limits supporters.

Chapter Three

The Power of the Incumbents

*The Democrats and the Republicans have this distinction
on terms limits: Democrats say they're against term limits,
the Republicans say they're for them.
They have this in common: they both hate term limits.
The Democrats are just more honest about it.*
—Bob Novak, December 1995

The debate over term limits, and the movement of supporters it was able to attract, was initiated against a background of a fortress-like Congress, a place that was almost impossible to penetrate. The situation improved somewhat during the second part of the 1990s, but in the 1980s and early 1990s, if a representative decided to run for reelection, he or she would be almost certain to return to Congress. In addition to sending a discouraging message to all potential challengers, especially Republicans, such a situation is problematic from the point of view of democratic practice and theory.

The situation is problematic because it limits, actually or potentially, the number of competing candidates, thus affecting the democratic principles of "freedom of choice" and "candidate chances of being chosen" (see chapter 2). But are these choices really free? Do elected representatives really represent their voters? Modern political theory provides negative answers on these two counts. In effect, the amalgamation of voters' preferences is not reflected in the choices (i.e., the representatives) society attains. This chapter explains why. The disproportional power of incumbents vis-à-vis their challengers is but part of this disturbing effect.

Based on some of the findings developed by rational choice theorists, we first address the concept of freedom of choice. We then move to explain why incumbents have such a huge built-in advantage in their electoral competition over their challengers. For this we employ conceptual tools developed by the spatial models theories. Finally, we present a set of practical "barriers to entry" designed by "insiders" to prevent "outsiders" from penetrating into the political system. Note that in the above presentation we employ conceptual tools familiar to most students of rational choice theory. Hence, our net contribution in this chapter rests in the realm of interpretation and relevancy to an actual political problem.

People's Freedom of Choice

The concept of "freedom of choice" is tossed around freely in democratic controversies, similar to the one generated around the issue of term limits. The fact is that voters are not always free to choose whomever they wish, and if they are, then their choices do not always reflect their preferences. This sound conclusion is the founding block on which rational choice theory rests.

The man accredited with this astonishing finding is Kenneth Arrow (1963). Arrow followed in the footsteps of the two great eighteenth century French mathematicians Condercet and Borda and the nineteenth century English genius Rev. Dodgson (alias Lewis Carroll) (Riker and Ordeshook 1973). Incorporating the so-called "paradox of voting" (see below) to his scheme, Arrow devised a theorem to prove that one could not arrive at social outcomes based on the preferences of the individuals involved without violating some essential democratic values. Properly, this finding is known as the impossibility theorem. Put differently: there is no social choice function (e.g., electoral method), actual or even imaginary, that can aggregate individual preferences and still produce results which are consistent with an even small set of democratic values.

What are these values? Prime among them is the so-called "universal domain," which states that any alternative (i.e., candidate) for a choice should be admissible, so long as individuals have preference over it—in other words, unrestricted freedom of choice. Other values include (a) consistency: if more people support a given alternative this should be reflected in the social choice, independent of irrelevant alternatives, which means that only those presented for a choice should be considered; (b) citizens' sovereignty: to protect the choice from outside interference; and (c) non-dictatorship: to protect it from the desire of one person. Every empirical or even imaginary voting system violates one or more of these values. To obtain consistent results, democracies, as we shall see below, usually restrict the scope of alternatives presented for a choice.

When the number of alternatives is not restricted and voters are asked to order them according to their preferences, then the paradox of voting prevails. Consider the following situation:

A group of voters, say N=11, are asked to order their preferences among three candidates: A, B, and C. They do that in the following manner: Five voters express a preference schedule that takes the ABC form (read: A in the first place, B in the second, and C in the third). A second group of five supports a BCA profile. And the third group, consisting of only one member, holds CAB. Clearly, the social choice, based on the preferences of the voters, is expected to be either the one supported by the first or the second group. It is, and it is not—let us see why.

In comparing the support given to candidate B against the support given to C, we learn that he obtains the support of the second group plus that of the first group who rank B higher than C. Ten people, then, preferred B over C and therefore, he should prevail as expected. We now position B against A. A wins by a margin of six to five, based on the strength obtained from his people plus the support of the single voter in the third group. Let's now reverse the order of presentation. Now C is being set against A and wins by a margin of six (the second and the third groups) to five. But when placed against B, the latter wins 10 to 1. As noted, this should be expected, for A and B initially obtained the largest support, and it was up to C, the pivotal candidate, to decide which of the two would prevail as winner.

Can C himself be the winner? The answer to this unlikely situation, where clearly a minority candidate wins the election, is affirmative. Let's see how. Place A against B. A wins by a six to five margin. B is taken out of the competition, and A is positioned against C. Now C, the candidate that initially obtained the support of only one member who placed him in the first place of his preference order, wins by a margin of six to five. This is indeed a disturbing outcome. To think that the social choice reflects the preferences of only one person, ignoring the sincere wishes of the majority of voters, goes against democratic understanding. Such outcomes, where A beats B, B beats C, and C in turns beats A, show that the logical property of transitivity, assisting individuals to order their priorities and make inferences, may not be applied at societal level. Such outcomes are also called "Cyclical Majorities," and while they affect our choices and introduce to them a certain measure of arbitrariness, it is not clear to what extent they distort our wishes (Niemi and Weisberg 1968; Demeyer and Plott 1970). On this, Riker (1969) commented that Arrow's finding is so dramatic that it forces us to reopen basic questions concerning our understanding of the functioning and the guiding norms that underlie liberal democracy.

Note that in the above example, the outcome changed every time that the order in which the alternatives were presented for choice was altered. This means that the order of presentation, not just the preference of the voters over the alternatives, affects the outcome. This is an obvious conclusion, for we know that voting schemes are basically mathematical formulas, and that a change in one of their components (read: term limits can become such a component) or in the way they are used would likely affect the outcomes. It also means that if there are some who could control the order of presentation of the alternatives, then they could also attain their desired outcomes. Here, among other places, is where the art of political manipulation finds its home (Riker 1986).

For example, suppose that in our earlier illustration of the eleven-member society, one of the members assesses that the outcome would favor the first group. To prevent this, he or she introduces the C alternative, causing different outcomes. Thus, control of the agenda, expanding or condensing the scope of the issues over which people express preferences, is the real stuff of politics. Riker, upon whose wisdom we draw heavily for the construction of this argument, best expressed this; he writes

> Outcomes are the consequences not only of institutions and tastes, but also of the political skills and artistry of these who manipulate agendas, formulate and reformulate questions, generate "false" issues etc. in order to exploit the disequilibrium of tastes to their advantage (1980:445).

Incumbent politicians, so it has been revealed, have an advantage in this area of political practice. They are successful in their bids over and over again, because among other things, they know how to control or how to adjust themselves to the relevant winning political agendas. But is not this fact that they are successful, over and over again, in and of itself a contradiction to that theoretical argument explained above? Is it not their ability to sustain their office for four, five, or even more terms, an empirical testimony to the tremendous consistency, not randomness, that results from the people's choices? It is, and the reason for this is that essential democratic values are being violated, and in particular the one that requires that no limitations be imposed on the scope and span of the alternatives presented for choice. No empirical democracy meets this demand.

This fact constitutes the cornerstone of the relatively new approach in modern political science known as the neo-institutionalist school. The scholars researching in this field promote the idea that what induces consistency in our choices, what makes for stable and durable outcomes, are the array of institutions in the polity (Doron and Sened 2001). These institutions guide political behavior, but more importantly, they limit the scope and range of the candidates being considered at any given point in time. In doing so, they reduce and often eliminate the possibility of the occurrences of cyclical majorities.

What are these stability-inducing institutions? In America, the reference is first and foremost to the Constitution. It generates a stabilizing effect, not just because of what is included in it—right or wrong, good or bad—but because it is so difficult to change (Buchanan and Tallock 1962). Hence, people's behavior and choices in the political arena must be adjusted to its dictates, as was shown in chapter 2. Limitations on the scope and range of the alternatives are attained not only by a formal set of explicit laws and regulations, but by other factors that generate the same effect. Three of these are discussed in the following section: the two-party system; the method of plurality voting; and the American political culture.

The Two-Party System

Nowhere in the Constitution has it been written that Americans should elect their representative by a two-party system. Indeed, since independence, there were often more than two parties presenting their candidates for election. In fact, quite often there were several parties whose candidates were competing at the same time for a variety of posts. Few amongst them, usually referred to as third parties or independent candidates (Abramson, Aldrich, Paolino, and Rohde 1995), materially affected the outcomes of general elections. Between 1832 and 1992, a total of thirteen third parties or independent presidential candidates received significant numbers of votes (around 5 percent) that directly affected the outcomes (Abramson, Aldrich, Paolino, and Rohde 1995). But, of course, there were many more candidates competing that did not fare nearly as well. For example, in 1836, because of internal divisions in the party, Whigs had three presidential candidates competing against the party's choice, Martin Van Buren. One of the most famous successful examples of third party candidates is Woodrow Wilson's Progressive Party. Since World War II there have been some prominent candidates competing with presidential ones who were, naturally, members of the two major parties. The first was George Wallace, the governor of Alabama, who challenged both the Republican Richard Nixon and the Democrat Hubert Humphrey in 1968. While he represented the extreme right, attracting mostly the Southern Democrats' votes, the other two were centrists. John Anderson believed in 1980 that he could do better than the incumbent, Jimmy Carter, and his principal challenger, Ronald Reagan. He could not, but he helped Reagan defeat Carter. Ross Perot, a billionaire who need not rely on contributions or government matching funds, made two unsuccessful bids for the presidency in 1992 and 1996. He certainly was instrumental in helping George Herbert Walker Bush out of office and helping Bill Clinton in. Wallace, Anderson, and Perot lost, but their candidacies affected the outcomes of the elections in which they competed; it increased the intensity of the electoral competition and, consequently, the number of people who turned out to vote. Presumably, many of the people who supported these third party candidates would not have voted without the option with which they were presented. Also, there are often some among the congressmen who identify themselves as Independents, not belonging to either the Republican or the Democratic parties.

Effectively, however, the electoral competition in the United States, for executive posts (e.g., president, governors) and for both federal and state legislators, is conducted between candidates representing the two major parties: the Republicans and the Democrats. These are not ideologically oriented parties in the European sense, but rather a federation of individuals and groups whose substantive and normative positions may be quite different even within each of these parties. The European political institution of "party discipline" is relatively ineffective in the United States. However, seniority in Congress serves as an important component in the decision to assign committees chairmanship positions (see chapter 5). While the practice of party discipline represents a binding agreement among party members to vote uniformly on given issues, each American congressman actually works on his own. Therefore, Richard Rose (1984) suggested counting 535 active political independent parties in Congress at any given time.

The voter's choice does not expand with such a count. Voters are usually faced with only two candidates. Walton (1980) called this situation: "the two parties monopoly," whereby each respective party must endorse its candidate. The selection of candidates is done at the party level, through primaries or other methods (Brams 1996). Only active party members are involved in this selection. There are no special qualifications to run for office, apart from those specified by the Constitution (e.g., age or place of residency). Often, when a serving politician expresses a wish to continue to hold the public post, no challenger will confront him or her. He or she will then be approved automatically by party members, who are often the activists working for that person.

The outcome of this process, which is familiar to most readers, is that two names are placed on the ballot. Candidates with little chance of winning would also have little chance of mobilizing the amount of resources and personnel needed to launch a fair competition. Candidates who are willing to finance their campaign with personal resources may improve upon these chances.

But to maintain the monopoly (or rather, duo-poly), members of the two parties collude and pass laws that put effective obstacles on the freedom of access and the bidding chances of third parties and independent candidates. Some of these obstacles, known as "barriers to entry," are specified below.

One way or another, then, the voters are usually faced with only two alternatives, and many times it is actually only one. This means that the practical consequence of the political system stands in direct violation of Arrow's universal domain condition, even if it induces stability in the polity.

The Plurality Voting Scheme

When there are two candidates, the winner obtains, by definition, the majority of votes. Basic electoral rules, Art. II, Sec. 1 of the Constitution, as modified by the 12th Amendment, specifies that a winning candidate must have a majority of the electoral votes. Indeed, if the voter turnout rate is less than 50 percent, which it often is, this majority, which is considerably smaller than comparative figures of other democracies (Powell 1986), may reflect the support of only a minority of the concerned citizens. From this perspective, over the last several rounds of presidential elections, because of a low turnout, the prevailing choice has represented only a small fraction of the American people, even when it was labeled a "landslide" (e.g., Lyndon Johnson vs. Barry Goldwater in 1964; Richard Nixon vs. George McGovern in 1972; and Ronald Reagan vs. Jimmy Carter in 1980.)

When there are more than two candidates, the outcome may be, from the perspective of democratic theory, even more bizarre, as a result of the voting scheme used in the United States. Suppose, for the sake of argument, that there are ten candidates. This could very well be a reality, when the primaries mechanism is enacted. To win, the victor needs no more than 11 percent, providing that each of the other candidates obtains less. He or she may become the choice of that party and accordingly be placed on the ballot against the choice of the other party. Note that in this hypothetical example, which may be quite reflective of real life situations, 89 percent of the voters did not vote for the winner. They thus may not turn out to vote in the general or the state elections, if they hold a sincere preference against their own party's chosen candidate; alternatively, they may come out to vote only if they wish to prevent the other party's candidate from being elected. Thus abstention from the electoral process or participation on the basis of negative motivation may characterize the act of voting. In this scheme, because they are usually better organized, incumbents challenged at their party primaries would usually fare better than their challengers when there are multiple candidates and low turnouts.

While the above illustration seems trivial for most who are aware of the prevailing differences that often exist between popular support and actual outcomes, few also acknowledge the effect synchronization of the election has on the outcomes (see more on this issue in chapter 5). In the American plurality system, because elections are not synchronized due to Constitutional dictates, a majoritarian effect is being generated. The local party organization is asked to contribute to election efforts every two years. It is asked to get involved in the local, state, congressional, and presidential electoral bids. It is possible, then, that the same small groups of organized activists are involved in all of these efforts. Hence, winning a senatorial race in a given state, for example, may improve the chances that another senator from the same party would also be elected by the same organization the next time. Therefore, many states go Democrat or Republican for many years, with both their senators and many of their representatives in the House belonging to the same party. However, if the elections took place at the same time, as they do in other democracies, then to win two seats in a two-party system, each party would have to recruit the support of at least 67 percent of the voters. In the prevailing system, the same group of voters that elected one senator would elect the other; they would be represented by two people and the rest of the voters by none.

Political Culture

Political culture is indeed a very difficult factor to define, even if is used frequently in the study of political phenomenon. But it is important to our intuitive understanding, for it captures modes of behavior, regularized practices that are internalized and performed by political actors in a given polity. These should provide an indication of the things included in the set of politically relevant items over which people express preferences, and those that are excluded from the set. Freedom of choice is thus affected by the specific contents of items defined by the polity's culture.

An extreme example will suffice to illustrate the effect of culture as a definer of the boundaries of the choice-set. For example, no one would seriously think to establish a political party whose platform would promote the eating of cows in the Indian democracy (Sen 1970). The offense of such an act against the feelings of the majority would be, presumably, much too great. Such a political formation would not materialize in India, irrespective of that country's constitutional position. Likewise, the sense of personal responsibility and the shame associated with public embarrassment of the Japanese politicians seems to be greater than in other political cultures.

Perhaps one of the most telling accounts of American political culture is given by the Frenchman Alexis de Tocqeville (1944), in particular, the description of the intense debates at public meetings conducted by volunteer associations of involved citizens. Many others provide references to such institutions of community-oriented direct democracy in early America. What was culturally established then is the close link between caring citizens and their representatives. The practice of writing letters to one's state senator or representative in the House and expecting to get a response is one expression of such a link.

Similarly, over the years several cultural, not legal, political traits have developed. In a two-person electoral competition, the loser usually goes home. This is often called, in game theory literature, a zero-sum situation (Ordeshook 1986) whereby the winner takes all, leaving the loser to find ways to cover unpaid campaign bills. All losers, who do not command personal resources, have to find ways to cover their campaign expenses. One of them, presidential candidate George McGovern (D-SD), turned to business following his defeat in 1972 and made the following statement after his motel folded: "I wish I had a better sense of what it took to [meet the payroll] when I was in Washington" (quoted in Fond 1991, 232). And this is the type of expertise a politician who could have been in a position of power, and whose decisions could have significantly affected American and global economy, brings to the post?

Tabarrok (1994), in a brilliant analysis of the various scholarly proposed explanations and rationales associated with the effects of term limits, which he finds unconvincing, offers one of his own to support the adoption of the idea. His explanation is essentially a cultural one although it is not presented in cultural terms. It goes as follows: let's not assume that voting against an incumbent is a close substitute to term limits. Instead, let's employ a different proposition that the longer one stays in power, the more likely that power will be abused. Therefore, the greater the expected rotation of power, the less likely that the present politicians would exploit their powers against others. To illustrate, if members of a coalition (i.e., any given group of politicians) are risk-averse because they know that a change of power is likely after some specified time interval of ruling, they will fear retaliation by others for their power abuses. Consequently, the present coalition would prefer to rotate power with rival coalitions and in this way share the spoils of governing rather than gamble upon winning or losing all political power for a lengthy period of time. Term limits introduce the certainty that power will be rotated after some time and therefore would produce less conflict-oriented and more cooperative politics.

Tabarrok then brings some empirical examples to illustrate his point. They include the rotation arrangement devised for Bosnia's presidency between the Croats and the Muslims, and the mitigating effects of whites' attitudes toward the blacks in South Africa, the further that regime moved on the route to power transformation. Of course, there are some other rotary apparatuses used in democracies. Switzerland uses one of the oldest one-year rotations for the service of its president; Israel used another for its prime minister between 1984 and 1988. And in general

Tabarrok alludes, albeit without mentioning it, to one specific form or mechanism of conflict regulation or of political arrangement used in divided societies (Nordlinger 1970), otherwise known as Consociational Democracy. But to obtain this, one needs more than a technical apparatus, such as term limits; one needs also a cultural shift, a change in the basic perception that people have regarding the ways politics is conducted in their societies.

In other words, Tabarrok is essentially suggesting a shift from the zero-sum condition that defines American politics to a positive-sum condition that permits political corporation. But in American politics, like in American competitive sports and in American business, the guiding motto has usually been: "There is nothing better than winning but winning itself." The single-member districts from which representatives are elected are a reflection of this winner-take-all attitude and practice. Furthermore, the competitive culture produced by the capitalist orientation is promoting risk-taking in all walks of life. The gambling entrepreneurs may gain the desired spoils; the losers may end up bankrupted. Term limits reflect this attitude: it is the "losing" public against the politicians. It is the traditional rivalry between outsiders and insiders, or between "us" and "them." At last count, the "people" won in twenty-two states (including Utah), but as chapter 2 showed, they were rendered "losers" on the national level.

Political losers, those who give up their posts to others, may plan a comeback, of course, but this would usually be to the same position over which defeat had been recorded in the first place. Like in professional sports and unlike the practice on the European Continent, going "down" in a political class (e.g., a senator running for the post of House representative) is not very familiar to American politicians. Neither is the European institutional practice of "shadow government," which is constructed after the elections by the losers who consistently produce criticism and alternative plans to those which are undertaken by the government.

And there are many more cultural traits that define political life in America. These include expectations for "clean" personal conduct of elected politicians; their church-going practices; their family (and, of course, personal) affairs; expectations for fulfillment of explicit promises, even when these were made during electoral campaigns; permission to provide spoils to winners' loyalists only up to a certain level, etc. Politicians' conduct on these and other matters are reported to the public on a regular basis, by the mass and local media, and by organizations, which were founded with the sole purpose of providing the public a direct "watch" over the performance of the representatives. In addition, many organizations have been formed to supply public service in the form of "analysis," "interpretations," or "policy directives." Two examples of such organizations are the liberal-oriented Brookings Institution and the conservative-oriented American Enterprise Institute. Information produced by these and other similar sources, and the ways it is presented in the electronic and printed mass media, in addition to the quality of the politicians' involvement in their community affairs (Fenno 1978), constantly affect voters' preferences. The quality of this information and its personal processing may determine voters' choices on the decisive day of election.

In light of the above, it may be easier to understand parts of the civic motivation that drove the supporters of the term limits movement. From a cultural point of view, term limits have been practiced in America since its independence. Politicians leaving office after only one or two terms (and with some acceptable exceptions, three) has been the norm, and an integrated element of the political-culture code. American voters needed very special circumstances not to retaliate against a bold circumvention of this code, as exhibited by the four-term tenure of FDR. Indeed, potential catastrophes at home caused by a deteriorating economy, hyperinflation, and high levels of unemployment, and dictatorial military threats from the outside (i.e., World War II), were the necessary unusual conditions. But when times became relatively normal, restoration of the cultural code was demanded. Because it was broken, it was fixed by legal means.

This is not the case with legislative term limits. Here there have been no special conditions in recent times that would justify breaking the code, and most of the men who violate it cannot be considered as "unusual" in any of the senses that Hamilton meant. They are simply clever politicians, unwilling to leave office and able to be reelected over and over again, irrespective of the quality of their performance in Washington D.C. They block newcomers with fresh ideas and energy. Some have become, over the years, institutions by themselves, institutions not necessarily compatible with the preferences of the majorities at home. Because of this, in the California Senate, for example, there is a member who has been in office since 1938 and has unkindly been labeled "the geriatric ward of California" (Schrag 1995:25). How these politicians are able to sustain their posts for so long is the topic we discuss below.

Of no less importance from a political culture point of view is the attitude elected officials hold toward public money. In America, where the individual citizen is defined to be the sovereign, the expectations are that public monies, the contributions of the citizens to the production of public goods, will be used efficiently and effectively (see also chapter 5). It is the expected task of the representatives to make sure that expenditures be properly supervised, utilized, and redirected to enhance public interest, however this term is defined (Redford 1958). When these expectations are perceived as not being met, the culturally-oriented definition and explanation of such failure is often "corruption." Term limits supporters often used the term "corruption" not to indicate a personal illegal conduct of a politician, which could easily be fixed, but as a substitute to a cultural or normative phenomena: abuse of power, detachment from the people, and insensitivity to their expectations. "When Government screws up, we Americans tend to invent new rules to fix the problem . . . to correct the maddening ineffectiveness and endemic corruption of Washington" (Lofdahl 1992). And why does Washington behave in a seemingly corrupt manner? The answer is that politicians stay too long in power and thus tend to forget who sent them there and whose interests they should serve. Consequently, they waste too many resources or direct them to places and people who do not deserve them, at least from the "people's" point of view. The term limits movement can thus be understood as the peoples' counter-cultural attack on politicians in general and those who serve in Washington in particular, because it "would help prevent life-long congressional careers and the separated Washington culture that goes with it" (Lofdahl 1992). It is a movement that does not promise a new world but that asks to bring back the "good" old values of self-reliance. Although its motif is based on negation of the prevailing political culture, it encompasses both conservative and liberal values, both strengthening the place of the individual in the webs of the American polity and opening new avenues and opportunities to marginal groups to move into the centers of political activities.

From a political culture point of view, the drive for term limits could thus also be understood as a democratic exercise in people's empowerment. And this, from the point of view of basic democratic theory, is not a "bad" thing in and of itself. Indeed, the trade-off is clear: it is between the adverse effects that may stem from a process of delegitimizing politicians and the benefits obtained by increasing people's participation in the decision-processes that shape their lives. An effective democracy should promote various forms of citizens' participation and needs not just rest on one form consisting of "informed" but "passive" citizens, as some have suggested (Almond and Verba 1963). The term limits movement is one important such alternative form of civic participation involving active and concerned people.

The Competitive Advantages of Incumbents

Once a politician enters an elective post that person seems to enjoy a tremendous competitive advantage over future challengers. This observation holds for many democracies including the American one. Some information will shed light on this phenomenon. In 1990, almost all incumbents who were challenged in congressional races were reelected. Four years later, the challengers were doing much better; 10 percent of this group were able to defeat incumbents. This small but significant improvement was not repeated in 1996. This time, incumbents' rates of winning returned to a high of 95 percent. These less than 10-to-1 odds are not attractive to any challenger; for it is clear that the cards must be stacked somehow in favor of the representatives of the "House."

In comparison, when competition is conducted over open seats, the chances of outsiders (women and minorities; see next section) are much higher. For example, for the 105th Congress, 70 percent of the women serving in the House of Representatives were elected in open seats. Likewise, 83 percent of the minority members of the House of Representatives were elected in open seats (America Back in Charge 1999). Put differently, rotations of power (i.e., seats changing their individual occupants, not necessarily seats switching to another party), are certain to take place in open seat elections to the House and to the Senate while they are highly unlikely in elections with incumbents to these two institutions.

Incumbents have advantage over their challengers due to several reasons. The simplest one could easily be explained as being a product of a statistical advantage. Assume that incumbents have some loyal followers. Now assume that both incumbent and his or her challenger are equally effective in all aspects related to the electoral competition. Under these assumptions, according to the binomial distribution, if there are 'n' informed voters and they vote randomly, half of their votes would go to the incumbent (P1=.5) and the other half to the challenger (P2=.5). The incumbent can expect half of their votes with a variance $P(1-P)/n = .25/n$. Therefore, as 'n' increases, the variance of the proportion of the voters voting for the challenger decreases. Given the first assumption, from a statistical point of view, organized groups of loyalists would have a decisive effect on the outcomes in favor of the incumbent. This also implies that in order to improve the chances for winning, the challenger also needs to attract groups of loyalists. These can usually be found in the two major parties and in organized associations (unions, churches, civic associations, etc.).

There are other reasons that incumbents have an advantage. Among them, two are most important: the candidates' ability to correctly position themselves at the median of the distribution of voters' preferences and the voters' tendency to minimize regret.

The Incumbent's Median Strategy

Much has been written about the wonders of the new groups of professionals, the "political strategists" who join campaigns around the world of democracies and guide their clients into victories. We seldom hear about their losses. The development of this new profession indicates that either politicians have come to realize that electoral campaigns are a business too serious or too complex to be handled by themselves, or that their ultimate goal does not necessarily reflect their sincere ideological conviction. The name of the political game must therefore be winning, and it is not foreign culturally to the voters.

Besides the resources needed for a campaign, the experience and knowledge acquired during earlier rounds is invaluable. Old mistakes will not be repeated, and new ones may not have similar damaging effects. It has been found that one of the reasons that explains why there are fewer women than men in high political posts relates to the fact that they tend to lower their political ambition after one or two campaign bid failures (Doron and Shoncker 1998). Hence, experience and even failures may become good guides to future victories. In this respect, just like in competitive sports, the psychological make-up of the politicians contributes to the determination of the outcome. Very few other "secrets" are left to be explained except for the so-called spatial position of the candidates.

A candidate can win a two-person race if he or she obtains at least 50 percent of the votes. To do so, the candidate must place him- or herself on the median point of voters' preference distribution. When the electoral competition is conducted over only one issue and between two people, the location of that point should be rather easy. It is not. Superficially, it seems that it is enough to locate the median position on the basis of data accumulated by surveys where voters are asked to express their positions over a given issue. Surveys, although effective tools in locating positions in a political issue space, are not always reliable (Doron 1998). They always leave, for example, a margin of statistical error. Sometimes the size of this error is what makes a winner a loser. The statistical findings express positions held by people on the day they were asked to respond, and these may be quite different from the positions that they will actually express on election day. Answers also include some proportion of "I don't know" or "I have not decided yet," next to sheer lies concerning true preferences and voting intents. In addition, it is not clear who will really come to vote and who will abstain.

Since the two candidates know that they should capture the median position, they move to that point by making appealing statements to the "median voters." Naturally, these statements are similar, often almost identical. Those potential voters who have difficulty in differentiating between the candidates' messages may abstain; they may become indifferent because both candidates represent their positions. Others who feel that the two median-driven candidates hold positions too far from their own may become alienated. They, too, may abstain (Downs 1957). Hence, the field of politically-minded citizens could be considerably reduced by those who abstain from voting for whatever reason. Those who are determined to vote but cannot distinguish between the candidates' positions may fulfill their civic duty and vote because of other factors. Their party affiliation or the personal attributes of the candidates may serve as such differentiating factors. Incumbents have an advantage over their challengers in these last two factors. They can also gain a better head start on their rivals in their movement across the issues' space. Before showing that, another important point must be made.

Elections are often conducted between more than two candidates and over more than one issue or dimension. When one candidate obtains advantage on one dimension, then the other should try to cancel that advantage by controlling another dimension. Outcomes of election conducted over more than two dimensions are difficult to anticipate, as proven so elegantly by McKelvy's theorem (1976). Better known as his chaos theorem, it states: "In a multi-dimensional spatial setting . . . there will be no majority rule empty-winset point. Instead there will be chaos—anything can happen, and whoever controls the order of voting can determine the final outcome." Thus, when more than two dimensions are involved, any result should be expected, just like the effects of the 'paradox of voting' presented above. Consequently, politicians attempt to condense the issue space to just one or two issues, over which voters are asked to express their preferences. Indeed, some voters may feel that these issues are not the most important for them, and hence the process of voting becomes less relevant to their well-being. They then would abstain too.

In other countries with different electoral rules (e.g., proportional representation), this last group of non-voters would create a pool of potential voters, attractive enough for someone to articulate new messages directed at them. This may lead to a formation of new parties that compete for representation. The Green parties, whose salient issue is the protection of the environment, and the extreme right parties in European politics, who use hate directed toward foreign labor to recruit political support, are illustrations of this type of political entrepreneurship (Shepsle and Bonchek 1997). In America, such an entrepreneurial outsider who appeals to alienated, even politically minded nonvoters, appears also from time to time on the political scene. It is thus very important to find out the spatial location of these entrepreneurs' target populations on the political map. The outsiders' entry point into a competitive political map may or may not affect the chances of one of the two principal candidates to gain political victory. Clearly, where run-off elections are not enacted, winning may be secured by less than 50 percent of the actual votes.

Incumbents have a built-in advantage over their challengers on three counts: in their spatial movement, party-affiliation, and personality. Incumbents do not have to make promises; they can show they have delivered. Whenever an issue rises that may develop into a future electoral problem, incumbents have the tools to address it. There are issues that may have a dampening influence on the incumbent's support and those that may positively be accredited to an opponent. In the first case, a policy remedy has to be delivered; in the second, those issues may be adopted and incorporated into the incumbent's program. Nixon, who "stole" McGovern's welfare ideas in 1972, and Clinton, who changed course in the middle of his first term from liberal to a more "centrist" president, are two illustrations of this practice. In general, the incumbent has more time to move into the median position if he or she is not already there. He can also generate, because that is his official duty, new issues on a daily basis. Thus the incumbent can easily capture the political agenda and divert public attention away from his or her challenger's campaign. Challengers' movements are reactive and must be sensitive not only to the wishes of the voters, but also to feelings of their activists and to the movement and actual policies of the incumbent.

Candidates' chances may be somewhat better if they represent a large organized party whose members are socialized to support anyone willing to carry their banner. Often, however, the contribution of the national party and its leaders are not relevant to local competition. What is relevant is the local organization, and this may be one that is entirely staffed by the incumbent's people. They, people whose livelihood and career depend on it, would make sure that their personal condition would not be changed for the worst. They are the party, sometimes even "the machine" (Norton 1949), that would see to it that their boss is elected, over and over again.

Incumbents also have advantages over their challengers on personal factors. This may be a surprising observation because personal attributes are not an objective matter; they are merely in the eyes of the beholder. Hence, it is unlikely that challengers would be disadvantaged relative to incumbents on this matter, or at least would not be perceived similarly. But they are, and we next provide an explanation for this interesting effect.

Minimization of Regret

Voting on issues and people to be representatives is an important civic act; for many it is their only voluntary civic act. Naturally, they would like to do it well. They would like, as when they face the decision of buying a car, to make no mistakes. They would therefore try to minimize the possible regret that may be associated in the future with the consequences of their choice (Doron and Harris 2000). This observation, which is pessimistic in essence, is captured by the concept of Nash Equilibrium (Nash 1950). This says that although one's choice may lead to better states, it can also be conducive to a much worse one. And to avoid the horns of this potential dilemma, people tend to choose the known over the unknown. Or, as the old Irish saying goes: "We prefer the devil that we know over the devil that we do not know." Indeed, the incumbent is that known devil.

To use an analogy from the field of marketing of consumer goods, the difference could be likened to that which exists between "experienced goods" and "search goods" (Ferguson 1974). The former (e.g., bread) one buys because one already knows their quality, but for the latter (e.g., can of sardines), because one cannot taste or see the nature of the product, one takes a chance on the credibility of the producer. To sustain this perceived credibility, producers (or sellers) must keep a tight quality control over their products, offering exactly the same quality each time. Hence, the concept of canned food or hotel chains that offer the very same taste and quality of service everywhere and every time, so as to reinforce the loyalty of the consumers to the product. Hence, greater investments in advertisement are required for search goods than for experience goods because one can tell in the latter about the quality of the product by just seeing or testing it. One has little way of knowing a priori how good a search good is going to be (Nelson 1974). While both types of producers compete with others over market shares, experience goods need considerably less promoting, just the knowledge that they exist and where to get them is enough.

The incumbent is the experienced entity, and the challenger the search one. Hence, the latter needs much more time and resources (which they often do not have) to introduce themselves to the voters. No wonder that, together with the demand to limit legislative terms, there is also an associated demand to enact campaign finance reform. It helps if the challenger has money (like the billionaire Ross Perot) or if he or she begins the electoral bid with some previous public exposure obtained in other areas (e.g., sports or movies).

Consequently, when faced one against the other, the incumbent has one personal attribute which is most important to the voter and which cannot be matched by the challenger: the certainty projected by experience. With him or her things cannot be much worse than they are now; with the new one: who knows? People gamble on the novice when things get really out of hand, if their perception is that whatever the future yields must be better than what is being experienced in the present. There are other mechanisms to minimize the possibility of such occurrences, and they are presented in the next section.

Barriers to Entry

Insiders have an advantage over outsiders because they constantly set up many of the rules that define the political game. When the prevailing political situation is consistent with their interests, then insiders work to preserve it. When it changes, creating potentially adverse effects on their chances of reelection, they move to put matters back on the right track. It is difficult to expect that active politicians, aiming to be reelected, would design rules that may reduce the advantages they already hold in the political arena. Some of these structural, mental, and formal advantages—the barriers to entry—were already discussed. For completion, in this section we concentrate on a few more. These include the selection process of the candidate, the availability of campaign resources, and the costs of voting.

The Candidates' Selection Process

It was mentioned in passing that "objectively" the challenger's odds of winning are not very attractive. These odds are sufficient reasons to leave most politically ambitious people to watch voting returns from the comfort of their homes. In fact, the real odds are even lower if we compute the probability of coming in first in the primaries' bid for each of the major parties. Suppose these ambitious individuals do not have the patience to wait until an incumbent would be willing to step out and leave the field for an open race. Is becoming an independent candidate an option to bypass the two parties and make a bid for the seat? Formally the answer must be positive; in reality, however, few have been successful in using this political route. The two large parties thought of ways to block the third option possibility. Both cooperate in all fifty states to discourage the growth of outsiders.

In Pennsylvania, for example, third party candidates for statewide offices must obtain the signatures of thirty-six thousand registered voters within a three-week period (Parenti 1988:177). Texas requires that the signers for independent candidates not be registered voters or not have cast a vote in the preceding presidential election; they also must recall their eight-digit voter identification number. A minor party must pay 10 cents for every signature it submits in Florida. Other states have similar restrictions, ranging from filing fees to forfeiting the rights to participate in other parties' primaries.

In British politics, potential candidates initiate their entry into politics by themselves, or the local or national party organization recruits them. They go through interviews, and if found ideologically and personally qualified, they receive their political assignment. When this happens, the entire party, in effect, endorses the candidate (Maor 1992). In contrast, in the United States, where the right to be elected is grounded in the

Constitution, anyone may become a candidate of that or the other party, so long as that person meets the minimal inclusive qualifications specified in the Constitution. So anyone can compete in the primaries of a major party without having to show a record of past activities, loyalty, or, for that matter, anything. The field on which the political game is played may thus be filled with many teams, one who may have a built-in advantage and the others each cutting into the others' zone. In such circumstances, it is difficult to make an educated assessment concerning who has the best chance of winning. Therefore, the excitement which usually characterizes campaigns and which is ignited by perceived achievements, and the consequential contributions to finance operations, may be put on hold until the field clears out and a potential winner is identified. Again, the known candidates, the ones best organized—the incumbents—would most likely prevail as winners, if at all challenged. The "universality" of the right to be elected, therefore, gets lost in the process of candidate selection.

The Availability of Campaign Resources

General elections are a defining but expensive feature of democracy, and therefore the citizens are required to contribute to this through their taxes. In other democracies such as Germany, where laws concerning the financing of elections are developed, the state finances candidates' electoral bids quite generously. In the United States, in contrast, these laws are not well developed, thus providing an additional competitive advantage to incumbents.

According to the Federal Election Act of 1974, public funds are equally divided between the two parties. These include matching funds for primary campaigns and national conventions. Essentially, then, candidates must first show that they are able to generate money before requesting that public funds match theirs. This practice creates a disadvantage for those who cannot or will not use their own resources to finance campaigns. Hence, those who have the money or can recruit it through contributions have a clear advantage over others. Moreover, the system of financing is designed to help the candidates of the two major parties. Third-party candidates can receive public finance only after the elections and only if they gain at least 5 percent of the votes (Walton 1980:176-78). Consequently, political entrepreneurs who wish to compete in the general election are discouraged from competition by those stipulations.

Three groups are usually the benefactors of the above system of campaign contributions: rich people, people whom the party endorses, and "insiders." The larger the relevant target voting population, the more resources are needed to reach it. Hence, rich people can buy time slots on the electronic media (which are not free as they are in other countries), produce the paper material, and cover their travel expenses with their own resources. The party is another source. In many ways, its most important functions have been to endorse candidates and serve as an address for the mobilization of resources. Once the party endorses a candidate, all affiliated individuals and groups are invited to contribute to the campaign. The candidate needs only to show that he or she has the potential to move up the campaign trail on his or her own, until the decisive stage. When the race is over an open seat, this kind of party endorsement is very important. When the race is not over open seats, the insiders—the incumbents—are at a great advantage, as explained above.

PACs (Political Action Committees) give nearly eight times as much money to incumbents than to challengers (Maisel 1990; Abramowitz 1991). Why? One possible explanation is similar in spirit to the so-called "captive theory of regulation" advanced by Stigler (1971) and others. Accordingly, the relationship and familiarity established over the years between politicians and special interests produce some form of exchange. Special interests would make sure that supportive politicians would have the necessary means to continue their jobs; the politicians would reward such support with favorable legislation. This durable relationship is quite disturbing in other fields, for instance, diplomacy. There, to understand and to be effective, an ambassador serving in a foreign country for a long time may gradually internalize the culture, values, and consequently even the interests of the host country and attempt to advance them at home. They become "localized." This is when ambassadors should be replaced. Term limits are said to produce such an effect.

It is not only money. Accesses to venues where candidates can present themselves to the voters are also important. Here is a testimony of Rep. Bob Inglis (R-SC) on this matter. During his first campaign for the U.S. House in 1992, running against an incumbent, he was faced with all sorts of problems. While the incumbent was invited to "factory after factory, workplace after workplace, event after event," Inglis's campaign "had to bite, pinch, scream, and kick to get invited to one factory." As an incumbent, he is invited to places all the time. And resources important for political campaigns also include time available for the candidates. On this Inglis recalled that when he was running as a challenger, he campaigned during the days but had "to spend his nights working at his law practice to keep his billing hours up to support his family." The incumbent, on the other hand, was given a month recess from Congress to come home and campaign full-time (http://www.abic.org/tlqa.html, interview with Bob Inglis, 26 June 2000).

Hence, the relative lack of a developed set of laws regulating the conditions under which candidates compete and elections take place becomes a barrier to the entry of the new ones into the political system. It perpetuates a situation of gross inequality in the electability chances of people who supposedly have an equal right to be elected, formally but unrealistically provided by the Constitution. To think that the insiders would do something to "correct" this situation is politically naive.

But even if there is a will, is there a way? The answer to this is very difficult. If one sets spending limits, equalizing the amount of resources competitors are permitted to spend during their election campaigns, then in fact one provides an advantage to the incumbent. This is because challengers have to spend more than incumbents just to break even. Incumbents have brand-name recognition. They have ready-made organizations working for them. They have spent years doing favors for their voters: here they produce passports, there they replace social security checks, and in other times they host visitors coming from their home districts to the capital. In every significant event occurring in their districts, their pictures are taken by the media next to those of the other elected officials: governor, the mayor, or the senator. In fact, incumbents use public resources to campaign all the time, even when no one defines their political activities as "campaigning"; during election times they just intensify what they regularly do. Challengers appear mostly during the actual campaign times that usually last no longer than one year. To equalize their spending, one would have to either limit the ability of the incumbent to meet his or her political duties or extend the time span in which a challenger could enjoy public support (e.g., in the form of matching funds). The first option is inadmissible from a normative point of view, for it goes against our understanding of the functions of representation. The second option is not practical, for challengers make up their minds and declare their candidacy based on their assessment of their chances only after they gather some relevant information about their competitors' performance and only after they obtain the formal endorsement of their parties. For that reason, it is not surprising to find out that in America, even ambitious politicians with sufficient resources shop around for an open seat race where they might have a reasonable chance of winning.

The Costs of Voting

Barriers to entry need not be reflected only at the politicians' end of the game; advantages may be generated by rules that guide voters' political behavior. Consider the individual costs of voting. If it is personally high for the individual, then he or she may decide to abstain from it. And if low turnouts are consistent with the interests of serving politicians, it is difficult to imagine that they will do much to reduce these costs. For example, declaring Election Day as sabbatical instead of conducting it on a regular working day, providing free transportation to voters from any place in the country—as the Italians do—to their designated voting booth, or changing the date of election to a more comfortable season could make a great difference in voting turnouts. But if the idea is to keep the percentage of voter turnouts low, because it favors the "insiders," none of this will materialize.

On the contrary, in some places the idea is to keep the turnouts as low as possible. For if voters come to the booths, politicians would most likely lose their positions. A typical yet bold example: the Alabama state legislator passed a "reidentification" law requiring counties with a concentration of low-income, anti-Reagan voters to register at inconvenient hours in obscure locations, with hostile officials presiding over the process. Since many poor blacks were without transportation and many were still economically dependent on whites, the result was a marketed decrease in African American registration (Parenti 1988:187). Abramson and Aldrich (1982), in observing the decline of electoral participation in America, were not looking much into the mechanisms devised to bring the voter turnout percentage down, but into its effects. They argue that since minorities and the poor vote in lower numbers, politicians tend not to pay attention to them. This, in turn, convinces these non-voters that the system is not responsive to their needs (Abramson and Aldrich 1982:519). Therefore, because there is no reason to vote, those most in need of the political system continue to stay out of the voting booths. Consequently, as Powell showed (1982; 1986), the American democracy has not ranked among the highest in terms of electoral participation of its citizens compared to other Western democracies. Someone has, presumably, a definite interest in prolonging this situation.

The calculus of voting is very simple. It has to do with the person's evaluation of the probability of materially affecting the election, the intensity of his or her like or dislike of the competing candidates, and the satisfaction of participating in an important democratic process (Riker and Ordeshook 1973). Of course, the more people who participate in the election, the less the objective probability that an individual would materially affect the final outcomes. And if either or both candidates do not provide sufficient reasons to like or dislike them, as explained in the context of the spatial analysis presented above, then voters' incentives to participate in the process are considerably reduced. Indeed, given this, some, including Tullock (1967), have proposed that it becomes irrational to vote. The perception of citizens that it is their duty to vote regardless of the results improves matters somewhat but does not significantly alter the belief that, for many voters, the personal costs of elections are greater than their perceived benefits. Therefore, many voters stay at home, which is fine with the insiders.

The costs of processing politically relevant information is another type of cost that generates disincentives to vote. We have already mentioned the risk-averse attitude of voters regarding new candidates. But often voters are asked, depending on the strategic plans of the candidates, to choose on the basis of too little information or too much of it. In the first case, the campaign is diverted to topics relating to the personality of the candidates and not to their positions over the relevant issues. In the second case, the public is asked to select candidates for many posts and express preferences over many policy issues. This requires some learning, analyzing, and data processing capabilities, attributes not found in abundance among many voters. The direct democracy scheme whereby citizens are occasionally asked, in way of referendum, to support or oppose a certain issue (e.g., term limits) requires considerable measures of learning and understanding. In Switzerland, for example, where this method is used, the fatigue factor generated by the rapid turning to the public to express preferences is conducive to a very low rate of actual participation (Powell 1982). This factor also has its definite effects in the United States. Positions are presented in an ambivalent way to purposely mislead voters (Downs 1957; Alesina and Cukierman 1990), or they are not addressing the important policy issues relevant to the welfare of the voters. Rather, positions are often presented in a media-type dramatic manner (e.g., they concern personal conducts of candidates in their youth, their family or extra-family affairs, etc.). In addition, there is often only a weak relationship between the candidate's ability to get elected and his or her skills of governing or of sincerely representing the preferences of the voters. This is all known to voters, albeit intuitively, and therefore it is not surprising that many choose not to participate in what should perhaps be considered the most important democratic event.

Note that those who stay at home and refrain from participating in the elections are not necessarily politically indifferent. They abstain from the prevailing political game because its existing rules or lack of proper rules make it difficult for them to play a meaningful game. Consequently, they ask to alter the rules of the game or, more precisely, to reduce the disproportional powers of the incumbents. They offered the device of legislative term limits. But in 1995 the Supreme Court ruled that the methods of limitation used by the states had been unconstitutional. To change, reformers need to move on the very difficult process of introducing a constitutional amendment. Since this way is so difficult, the option that remains is to keep the issue alive at the state level, to demand term limits for state legislators. To the analysis of this endeavor we turn in part two.

Part Two

TERM LIMITS AT THE STATE LEVEL

The Supreme Court decision in 1995 that defined as unconstitutional the initiatives taken by the states to limits the terms of their representatives in Washington sent a major blow to the members of the movements that promoted this idea. This blow, however, did not kill the idea; it merely redirected the reformers' energy to the state level.

This part includes three chapters. In chapter 4 we trace the activities of the various movements at the state level. We provide information on the steps that led three states to adopt term limits in 1990 and others that followed suit later. We also explain some of the reasons for the partial success in these states and others that contributed to the movement's failures to obtain positive results from their point of view. Three states receive special coverage: California, Colorado, and Massachusetts. Following the step-by-step development in these states provides a reasonable indication of the difficulties involved in enacting political reform at the state level.

Chapter 5 is a conceptually analytical one. It is presented against the background of the developments that occurred at the state level. It analyzes the concepts of experience, efficiency, and effectiveness, and of the two meanings of the time factor (cycles and synchronization) as they relate to term limits at the state level and in general to elections. The analysis shows that it is often difficult to assess the potential effects of term limits. In some cases one can expect this policy to improve the performance of the politicians; in others, one should not.

Finally, Chapter 6 presents an in-depth case study of term limits in the state of Michigan. We not only supply a general accounting of the situation, as we do in Chapter 4, but we also base our analysis on interviews with those people who were directly involved in one phase or another of the process by which term limits have been implemented.

Chapter Four

States' Legislative Term Limits

*The number of the citizens makes it convenient
for a number of persons to enter an office;
it permits some of the offices to be held
only once in a life-time, and others (though held more than
once) to be held again only after a long interval.*
—Aristotle, Book IV, Actual Constitution and their Varieties

The actual workings of state governments have never been exactly parallel to the similarly structured federal government. After the Civil War resolved the issue of sovereignty in the American Federalist scheme, a century of federal dominance in American politics took place. It was a period when the federal government exercised more and more power at the expense of the states. Its growing power culminated in President Franklin Roosevelt's New Deal during the 1930s, which led the federal government into policy areas that had previously been reserved for the states. Also, the executive branch has historically dominated politics and policymaking at the state level much more than at the federal level. Throughout much of American history, state legislatures have been part-time, poorly staffed, unprofessional, and politically weak (Moncrief and Thompson 1992:2).

The past half-century has seen a dramatic change in the makeup and power of state legislatures. This came about largely as a result of a loosely organized legislative reform movement in the 1960s and 1970s. Its goals were to make state legislatures more powerful and professional, and a more equal partner with the executive branch in policy and political affairs. One of the greatest vehicles for this change in state legislatures has been the elimination of many constitutional limitations. In 1940, only four states—New York, New Jersey, Rhode Island, and South Carolina—had legislatures with annual sessions; by the early 1960s, the number of states with annual sessions grow to nineteen; by the 1990s, forty-three held annual sessions (Pound 1992:10). Also, many legislatures have been given the power usually reserved for governors to call themselves to a special session.

Another significant constitutional change for many state legislatures has been the relaxation of limits on legislative salaries. In 1970, almost half of the states could change salaries only by amending their constitutions. Today, only five need to amend their constitutions for legislative salary increases (Rosenthal 1998:59). It is now possible in many states for legislators to rely entirely on the salaries they earn in government for their income.

These two changes in state constitutions have had the effect of making the position of state legislator more time-consuming and rewarding, and making a career out of being a state legislator more possible and appealing.

Perhaps the greatest change in giving more political power to state legislatures has been in their staffing. The increase in professional staff support that occurred in the 1960s and 1970s has helped make state legislatures more autonomous in their ability to obtain knowledge, conduct research and oversight, and handle the more administrative aspects of governance. The National Conference of State Legislatures has estimated that since the 1960s, the permanent staff of state legislatures has nearly quadrupled (Moncrief and Thompson 1992:201). State legislatures, with increased staff support, greater salaries, and longer sessions, have now become a much stronger actor in state politics than they were only thirty years ago.

A New Breed of State Politician

All of these changes in state legislatures have contributed to what is often called legislative professionalization. But, as Alan Rosenthal argues, the term is somewhat ambiguous: professionalization can refer to either the attributes of the body of legislature itself or to the qualities of individual legislators (Rosenthal 1998:54-55). Professionalization in a legislature means essentially the strengthening of the institution, giving it greater capacity to perform in the political arena. But professionalizing legislatures has had the effect, perhaps unintended, of encouraging careerism in individual legislators. A "new breed" of legislators emerged with modern state legislatures, those who, quite simply, consider their main occupation to be that of a legislator. Legislative professionalization, of both the legislature and the individual legislator, may have achieved some of the goals of the legislative reform movement of the 1960s, including more balanced power relations in state government, increased legislative efficiency, and more legislative policy analysis. But there may have been some undesired effects as well. The late 1980s and early 1990s saw an erosion of confidence in state legislatures and government in general. After so swift a modernization period, what has followed can actually be thought of as a reaction to relatively sudden changes, a backlash against the legislative modernization thought necessary only three decades ago (Rosenthal 1998:67).

There are several reasons why the public has become increasingly dissatisfied with Congress and state legislatures, and, generally speaking, the state of American politics. Several factors have contributed to a lack of faith and loss of confidence the American public has in its elected officials. For instance, certain political and historical events like the Vietnam War and the Watergate scandal have doubtless contributed to a loss of respect for elected officials. Not only had they made the wrong choices from the point of view of many, they also seemed to be lying to the people. The social unrest that spread over the American cities is partly the outcome of politicians' misconduct. Also, during the 1970s, a struggling economy at the national level, particularly in states like California and New York, did no good for the public's faith in government.

Aside from these events, the modernization of state legislatures may have had a more direct impact on the public's increasing disapproval of government and its officials. Legislative reform has made state legislatures more adept in the political arena; they now have generally greater policy analysis and development skills, more oversight ability, and are less at the mercy of the executive branch (Pound 1992:21). Yet professionalization has also brought with it an increase in lobbying and political action committees (PACs), greater legislator independence, and a decline in the authority of legislative leadership (Evans 1996; Sabato

1984). The greater number of professional legislators who see their position as an elected official to be their primary occupation might be more concerned with getting reelected than a true "citizen-legislator" would be, and they may devote themselves almost constantly to a perpetual reelection campaign. The cumulative effect of these changes is the perception that state legislators are more distant and remote from the people, more concerned with the affairs of special interests, and more concerned with their own ambition.

A Time for Political Change?

If the 1960s marked the beginning of a period of great change in state legislatures, with them becoming more powerful and professional, then the 1990s mark the beginning of another period of great change in state legislatures. This time, the movement is toward weakening and making the state legislatures less professional. Unlike the reform movement of the 1960s, which was led by academics, the media, and legislators themselves, this new push for change has come from a demanding public increasingly unhappy with these newly professional, "reformed" legislatures. Turnover is an area where one can easily see a change in state legislatures. In California, for instance, turnover in the state assembly between 1972 and 1990 averaged 20 percent; since 1990, it has averaged 36 percent. In Michigan, 76 percent of the representatives in the state house have been serving for less than a decade. The 1998 election in the Michigan House saw 64 out of 110 new members being elected (*Detroit News*, 8 November 1998). If one looks at state legislatures around the country, one finds that only 28 percent of all state senators have been serving for more than ten years, while in state houses the percentage of long-serving representatives is even smaller, at 16 percent (Rosenthal 1998:72). This turnover, however, is one of the symptoms of the de-institutionalization of state legislatures in recent years, not its cause.

According to Rosenthal, the "major de-institutionalizing force" in recent years has been the term limits movement. This movement was not operating in a vacuum. The political entrepreneurs that led it in the various states, financed by people like Kansas oil billionaires Charles and David Koch (Schrag 1995), were exposed to the old controversy over the issue and to its practical implementation at the presidential and the city level. Chapter 1 discussed the presidential term limits. The following pays some attention to the municipal level.

Although it is difficult to trace the developments in this diffuse area, it is known that term limits were imposed in some local places as early as the mid-nineteenth century. Even in modern times, some very large cities had term limitation long before it became a salient issue on the national and state political agenda. Philadelphia, for example, a city with a population of more than 1.5 million people in the 1990s, passed term limit restriction by a council vote as early as 1951. Perhaps the councilmen in this city reasoned that what was good for the president could also be good for them. El Paso, with a population of more than half a million people, also used its council vote to pass a term limits resolution in 1977. While term limits went into effect on the state level only in 1992, several major cities whose populations are larger than that of some small American states enacted election and forced limitations two, three, or four years earlier. They include: San Francisco and Wichita (1988); Dallas, Phoenix, and San Antonio (1989); Kansas City, Anchorage, and San Jose (1990); and New Orleans, Houston, Jacksonville, and Cincinnati (1991). In 1992, when term limits moved onto the agenda of several states and onto the national level, San Diego and Honolulu joined the troops. The biggest prizes for the idea advanced by the movement came later in 1993. During that year New York, Los Angeles, and Washington D.C. adopted term limits for their elected officials. Not surprisingly, in almost all places, the closer the adaptation of term limits in the local level to that in the states' level, the greater the popular support for its implantation at the municipal level. Interestingly, term limits on the local level were adopted even in places where the state and the national organization were not successful. It is difficult to know how many cities in the United States are currently enforcing term limitation on their elected representatives, but the number exceeds several thousand.

These developments could not escape the state-level term limits entrepreneurs, of course. In the 1990s, twenty-one states enacted term limits laws. The popularity of term limits can be measured by looking at two things. The first is the large majorities by which citizens in several states voted for term limits for their elected officials, and the second is the electoral defeat of term limits in only two small states where the issue was on the ballot—Mississippi and North Dakota. Currently, these new laws directly affect close to half of all state legislators. These simple facts are a testament of sorts to the power and success that the term limits movement had in the 1990s.

The Implementation of the Term Limits: The First States

In 1990, Colorado, Oklahoma, and California became the first states to pass term limits laws for their state legislators. The issue was decided on a referendum ballot in each of the three states. In Colorado, the measure was approved by 71 percent of the voters; in Oklahoma, 67 percent; and in California, only 52 percent. In Colorado and California, state senators were limited to two four-year terms in the senate; Colorado, however, limited state representatives to four two-year terms, while California's limit for the State Assembly was three two-year terms. Oklahoma's limits for lawmakers were unlike those of both Colorado and California; they allowed for a longer stay in office as shown in Table 4.1 below. These three term limit referenda that were approved in 1990 were a harbinger of things to come; by 1996, eighteen more states would pass term limits laws in referenda, and one state, Utah, would pass legislative term limits through the normal legislative process (see Table 4.2).

Oklahoma was the first state to pass state-level term limit laws. In September 1990, two-thirds of voters approved a term limits measure that would come to seem modest by later standards. A twelve-year limit was set for all state legislators (representatives and senators). A legislator was allowed in any combination of offices, as long as the twelve-year limit was not exceeded. The restriction to twelve years is hardly a constraint for most legislators, because twelve years is longer than the current average term of office. Like many innovations in policy and politics, the first experiment with the issue was modest, its value mostly symbolic. Later, state and federal term limits would become more stringent.

Table 4.1. Term Limits in the First States, 1990

State	Limit of Term	Percent Approval	Year of Effect
California	6 years in Assembly	52	1998
	8 years in Senate		2000
Colorado	8 years in House	71	2000
	8 years in Senate		2000
Oklahoma	12 years total for Legislators	67	2004

Source: Compiled from data from the states.

Colorado and California were the next to pass state term limits laws. In 1990, 71 percent of Colorado voters approved a state constitutional amendment to limit their state legislators' term of office. It was also the first state to limit their congressional delegation's term of office. Consequently, eighteen out of the sixty-five legislators were already affected by this new ruling. In the same year, Californians approved the "Political Reform Act of 1990," which added a section to the state constitution limiting the terms of state legislators as well as those of a number of other state public officials. In 1992, Californians approved the "California Term Limitations Act of 1992," which imposed ballot restrictions for U.S. Representatives and Senators if they had already served a certain number of years. Sixteen of the legislators have already lost their posts due to term limits (Steelman 1998).

It may still be somewhat premature to attempt to study conclusively how term limits have affected policymaking in Colorado, California, and Oklahoma. But certain effects regarding the makeup of the legislature and the changes in the political process have been felt. Let us have a closer look at California.

The term limits proposition in California was adopted and went into effect, but not without legal difficulties. The proposition limited state senators to two terms, state assembly members to three terms, and several executives to two terms. The proposition declared that lack of term limits created "unfair incumbent advantages" which "discourage qualified candidates from seeking public office and create a class of career politicians, instead of the citizens representatives envisioned by the Founding Fathers." Therefore, "term limits is necessary to restore a free and democratic system of fair elections, and to encourage qualified candidates to seek office."

In 1991, the constitutionality of Proposition 140 was challenged by several citizens, and the California Supreme Court concluded that term limits did not violate the plaintiffs' federal constitutional rights. Later, in 1995, Tom Bates, a former member of the California Assembly, filed an action alleging that lifetime term limits are unconstitutional (see *Bates v. Jones*, 958 F. Supp. 1446 [N.D. Cal. 1997]). The district court determined that Proposition 140 imposed a severe burden on Bates' 1st and 14th Amendment rights and was not tailored to advance state interest. The district court enjoined the enforcement of Proposition 140 but stayed its injunction pending appeal. The claim that the voters did not know what they are voting for, because Proposition 140 did not provide sufficient notice that it is for a lifetime ban, was rejected by the U.S.

Ninth Circuit Court. Consistent with the California Supreme Court, that court too agreed that Proposition 140 makes it clear that it asks for lifetime bans. This is because the wording of the Proposition, just like the wording of the 22nd Amendment (which limits the service of the president to only two terms), takes an absolute and not a relative form. They say that: "No Senator may serve more than 2 terms," and "No member of the Assembly may serve more than 3 terms." Consequently, the ballot access statute was reinstated.

The California State Assembly consists of eighty one-person districts. Of those eighty persons, twelve were elected in 1992 and therefore could not run in 1998. Out of these twelve (five Republicans and seven Democrats), eight were looking into a different political office (state senators, U.S. congressmen, and executive positions). Likewise, thirteen of the forty members of the State Senate had to quit their posts in 1998. Out of them, four were looking for other kinds of political jobs. In California, term limits profoundly affected turnover rates; after the 1996 election, none of California's eighty assembly members had more than four years legislative experience, and after the 1998 election, only a handful of the state senators had more than six (Schrag 1995:25). Eleven of twenty-seven assembly committees in California were chaired by freshmen; but during the early 1990s, no standing committee of California's state assembly was chaired by a freshman or even a sophomore legislator (Hodson et al. 1995:13).

Sheila Kuehl, an assemblywoman with three years' experience, and thus one of the most senior members of the California Assembly, said of the 1997 session, "We're still finding our way. We do not have a unified culture yet because so many people are new . . . we haven't even formed the relationships you form in the first year of college" (quoted in Schrag 1995:24-30). The National Conference of State Legislatures conducted a survey on California's assembly members elected since Proposition 140. It concluded that the most significant difference between the new term-limited legislators and their predecessors was one of experience; a much lower percentage of legislators elected after Proposition140 had served as legislative staffers. Their lack of knowledge and experience of the process of lawmaking "made them ill-equipped for anything but a passive role." (Hudson, et al.; quoted in Schrag 1995:24-30)

Yet, paradoxically, the composition of the Assembly has changed little since Proposition 140. In 1988, fifty-one Assembly members had been previously involved in politics; in 1997, the number fell only slightly, to forty-nine. Fifteen lawyers had been in the assembly in 1988; in 1997, there was only a small decrease to fourteen trained lawyers (Hyink and Provost 1998:113). This lack of great change in legislative composition was also demonstrated by Carey, Niemi, and Powell, who claimed that there were no "systematic differences in the backgrounds of the legislators from term-limited and non-term-limited states, whether we are talking about old-timers or newcomers" (Carey, Niemi, and Powell 1998:10).

More than one observer has noticed an increase in partisanship in California since Proposition 140 (Schrag 1995:24-30; Brewster and Kooperman 1997:59). It is reflected in the number of new position changes in the assembly and the number of special elections: In just a two-year period, 1995-1997, California had five assembly speakers, two senate leaders, and three recall elections, (Schrag 1995:24-30). There has also been a shift in power in the assembly from Democrats to Republicans, symbolized by the end of Democrat Willie Brown's tenure as assembly speaker in 1995. Brown had held this position longer than anybody (Brewster and Kooperman 1997:54). The legislators forced to leave office because of Proposition 140 have also begun what Peter Schrag has called a game of political musical chairs, finding work as lobbyists and consultants, which, in turn, has precipitated a power struggle in the assembly over the speakership and other top legislative positions (Schrag 1995:249; Caress 1996:671-678).

It is important to note that in California as well as in other states, the success of term limits has already been adopted as a campaign tactic. "Term limits candidates" compete against "non-term limit candidates" and use their pledge for term limits to gain an advantage among the voters. To illustrate: Roberts "Rob" Braden, a candidate for U.S. Congress, California, District 2, distributed among the district voters in 1998 a "Term Limits Declaration" signed by him on May 8, in the presence of two witnesses. In that declaration he pledged that he "will not serve in the United States House of Representatives for more than 3 two-year terms."

Colorado is another interesting state to look into regarding the operation of the term limits movement. There, the idea of term limits is pushed under the banner of the "Colorado Term Limit Coalition." By 1998, twenty-seven of the one hundred legislators were seeking new occupations. Moreover, the level of political competition intensified in several districts that were earlier considered safe seats. So, from a participatory point of view, the movement has accomplished its limited goal. Yet, as in other places, the movement has not stopped there. It continues to operate on several routes: providing the people information concerning its activities and plans (done by several means, including a Web site), protecting its achievements by legal means, and working on an initiative that could affect people's choices for their U.S. Congress representatives.

This Term Limit Initiative of 1998 provides a measure that any candidate seeking election to the United States Congress shall be allowed, but not required, to submit one of two specified term limits declarations. In the first, the candidate promises to limit his or her term in the House to three, and in the Senate to two. In the second, the candidate authorizes the secretary of state to place a ballot designation next to the name of candidate in all relevant places in which it is written: "Signed declaration to limit service to no more than [3 terms] [2 terms]."

Indeed, the movement has come into power. It has transformed the popular support it obtained into political power. In effect, it has become an interest group, using political techniques to advance its cause. Candidates seeking election must follow the rules dictated by the movement if they wish to solicit the support of the members of the movement. Moreover, the movement has undertaken a position of a public supervisor: it follows those politicians who support the so-called "phony" term-limit amendments, and it informs the public who is a sincere politician and who is not. Close public scrutiny over politicians' conduct is usually the responsibility of the press in a free society. But in Colorado, as well as in some other states, this became more like directly transferred political information. It may or may not affect voters' preferences regarding their political choices.

Spreading Term Limits to Other States

It is important to note that many of the changes in turnover and the resulting instability which have occurred in California and elsewhere will most likely be less profound in the state's upper house. In no state is a member of the senate restricted to fewer years of service than a member of the house or assembly, and often, as is the case with California and Michigan, state senators can serve two terms for a total of eight years in the state senate, as opposed to three terms for a total of six years in the state house. Thus the state senate should be less affected by term limits laws, especially since many state senators have prior experience in the state house (Hudson et al., Table 4.2). In states like Oklahoma, Nevada, and Utah the effects of term limits on the state senate will be even less severe. The law in those states restricts senators to twelve years of service, which is longer than the current average tenure for a state legislator.

Table 4.2 provides information on the types of term limits, the year of their implementation in each of the participating states, the size of the supporting majorities, and the years by which legislators would have to surrender their seats under the new ruling. Following the presentation of this information, we provide a kind of brief glossary of the states to evaluate the overall size and magnitude of this political phenomenon. Massachusetts is singled out for a longer presentation to get a feel for the difficulties the term limits movements encounter on their way to affecting a political reform.

In 1992, the term limits movement reached a summit of accomplishment: fourteen states, including Michigan, passed some form of term limits laws on their state and federal legislators. In Michigan, which receives our attention in chapter 6, Steelman reports that 67 of the 110 representatives were forced out. Arizona voters approved Proposition 107 in 1992, which amended the state constitution by limiting the number of terms that U.S. senators and representatives, state legislators, and other statewide elected officials may serve. The measure passed with 74 percent of the vote. Proposition 107 limited state legislatures to four consecutive two-year terms in either the state senate or house. During the same time, limits were also imposed on the governor, state treasurer, and attorney general.

Arkansas voters passed a constitutional amendment in 1992, limiting their congressional delegation and state legislators. For federal lawmakers, a lifetime ballot access restriction was enacted. After three terms in the U.S. House and two in the U.S. Senate, candidates were banned from the ballot. At the same level, the amendment limits members of the state house to three two-year terms and members of the state senate to two four-year terms. As a result of this ruling, 50 percent of Arkansas' house members were forced out (Steelman 1998).

In 1992, 77 percent of Florida's voters approved a constitutional amendment, commonly referred to as the "Eight is Enough" law. The amendment bans all state and federal lawmakers who have served eight consecutive years in one office from putting their names on the ballot. This amendment extended itself to include state executive cabinet officials.

Table 4.2 Term Limits in the States

State	Enacted	Limit on Term	% Approval	Year Effect	Method
Arizona	1992	8 years in Legislature	74.2	2000	Proposition 107
Arkansas	1992	6 yrs in House	59.9	1998	Const. Amd. #4
		8 yrs in Senate		2002	
Florida	1992	8 yrs in House	76.8	2000	Amendment #9
		8 yrs in Senate		2000	
Idaho	1994	8 yrs in House	59.4	2004	Proposition 2
		8 yrs in Senate		2004	
Louisiana	1995	12 yrs in House	76.0	2007	
		12 yrs in Senate		2007	
Maine	1993	8 yrs in House	67.6	1996	Question #1
		8 yrs in Senate		1996	
Massachusetts	1994*		51.6		Question #4
Michigan	1992	6 yrs in House	58.8	1998	Proposition B
		8 yrs in Senate		2002	
Missouri	1992	8 yrs in House	75.0	2002	Con. Amend. #12
		8 yrs in Senate		2002	
Montana	1992	8 yrs in House	67.0	2000	Con. Initia. #64
		8 yrs in Senate		2000	
Nebraska	1994*		67.7		Measure #408
Nevada	1994	12 yrs in Assembly	70.4	2008	Question #9
		12 yrs in Senate		2008	
Ohio	1992	8 yrs in House	68.4	2000	Question #2
		8 yrs in Senate		2000	
Oregon	1992	6 yrs in House	70.0	1998	Measure #632
		8 yrs in Senate		2002	
South Dakota	1992	8 yrs in House	63.5	2000	Con. Amend. A
		8 yrs in Senate		2000	
Utah	1994	12 yrs in House	No elect-ion**	2006	
		12 yrs in Senate		2006	
Washington	1992*		52.4		Initiative #573
Wyoming	1992	12 yrs in House	77.2	2006	Initiative #2
		12 yrs in Senate		2006	

Source: Washington Post, 2 June 1998, and other sources.
Note: Alaska, North Dakota, and New Hampshire also passed federal Congressional term limits before the 1995 Supreme Court ruling.
* Washington, Massachusetts, and Nebraska also passed term limits laws, but as of June 1998, the states' supreme courts ruled that statutorily imposed term limits are unconstitutional.
** Passed by state legislator.

Unlike most states that passed term limits laws for both state and federal officials, Missouri did not pass just one initiative dealing with both levels of government. Two measures were voted on, one dealing with state lawmakers and the other with Missouri's congressional delegation. The measures were approved by 74 percent of the voters. For the Missouri General assembly, no one may serve more than eight years in one house of the assembly, and no more than sixteen years in both. Once the limit has been reached, the ban is permanent. For their U.S. representatives, there is an eight-year limit; for U.S. senators, twelve years. The term limits provision for federal lawmakers in Missouri had a "trigger clause," which keeps that provision from going into effect until "at least one-half of the states enact term limits for their members of the United States Congress." Missouri is one of four states that had this "trigger clause." Of course, the 1995 Supreme Court decision defining as unconstitutional the limits imposed on U.S. congressmen makes the 1992 Missouri provision, as well as similar provisions made by other states, merely a statement of intent to be kept by the historical records.

Montana passed Constitutional Initiative 64 in 1992. Like Michigan's law, Montana's amendment prevents a candidate from appearing on the ballot for as many years as they have served once the limits have been reached. For state legislators, the limit is for eight years in any sixteen-year period (four terms out of eight for state representatives; two terms out of four for state senators). Nebraska voters also approved term limits for their state and federal lawmakers in 1992. In 1994, however, the Nebraska Supreme Court invalidated the law, ruling that the number of signatures initially collected to put the issue on the ballot was insufficient. After a new petition drive, the issue was on the ballot in 1994, and again the measure was approved. All state legislators are limited to two four-year terms in office. (Nebraska is the only state with a unicameral legislature. All legislators serve the same length of time). North Dakota is one of only two states to pass term limits only for its federal lawmakers; the other is Alaska. The limit set was twelve years for both U.S. representatives and senators. The amendment passed with only 55 percent of the vote, a considerably smaller percentage than average.

Like Missouri, Ohio had separate initiatives for its state and federal legislators. Ohio, in fact, had three initiatives: one for state legislators, one for federal legislators, and one for state executive officers. These all passed with roughly 66 percent of the vote. State legislators are limited to eight consecutive years in office. This is not a lifetime ban; a legislator can run for office after eight years of service if there is a span of at least four years between his last term of office and the term he or she is currently seeking. In Oregon, voters approved term limits for state and federal legislators and state executive officers. Three-term limits (six years) were enacted for state representatives, and two-term limits for state senators (eight years). The limit for total years of service in the legislature is twelve years. U.S. representatives were limited to three terms in office and U.S. senators to two terms. All limits in Oregon, for both state and federal lawmakers, were lifetime. Once the term limits were implemented, Oregon lost twenty-two of sixty representatives to that policy (Steelman 1998).

Sixty-three percent of South Dakota voters approved a constitutional amendment in 1992 limiting state and federal legislators and state executive officers. State legislators are limited to eight consecutive years. The limits for U.S. representatives were more relaxed: twelve consecutive years, or six terms in office. The state of Washington is an interesting case. Voters initially rejected term limits in 1990, but in 1992 the measure was approved. The law is a ballot access restriction. No incumbent can appear on the ballot for as many years as he or she has served in office. The restriction includes state and federal lawmakers, the governor, and lieutenant governor. Wyoming passed term limits laws in 1992 with 77 percent of the vote. For federal lawmakers, the limit was a ballot access restriction. For state legislators, it is strict term limits. For state house members, the limit is six years; for state senators, the limit is twelve.

Other states would pass term limits laws in 1994. As already mentioned, Alaska passed limits for its congressional delegation only— one of just two states to do so. Idaho, on the other hand, passed the most far-reaching of any of the states' term limit laws in November of 1994. Every level of government—federal, state, and local—was given some sort of term limits. Ballot access restrictions were imposed on U.S. representatives and senators, state legislators, municipal officers, and school board officials. Maine voters passed the "Maine Congressional Term Limitation Act of 1994" with 63 percent approval, restricting ballot access for U.S. senators and representatives for a certain number of years. Massachusetts and Nevada passed similar initiatives in 1994.

Utah is the only state where the legislature has itself passed term limits laws. The vote in the Utah state house on the "Utah Term Limitation Act of 1994" was fifty-six to seventeen. In the state senate, the vote was a bit closer, sixteen to eleven. It limits state legislators and state executive officers. For federal term limits, the Utah statute has a trigger clause requiring twenty-four other states to pass limits for their congressional delegations before Utah's takes effect.

It is interesting to follow the story of term limits in Massachusetts. The initiatives of LIMITS (the state organization that sponsored the Term Limits Law), began in 1991. That year 72,000 signatures were collected to support an amendment that would limit the term of the governor, attorney general, treasurer, secretary of state, auditors, governor's councilors, state legislators, and U.S. representatives to eight consecutive years in office, and U.S. senators to twelve consecutive years. In 1992 LIMITS collected more than fifty signed pledges from state legislators to approve a Constitutional Convention. But with court intervention, this option to amend the state's constitution was officially blocked. So by 1993, LIMITS decided to change its strategy and drafted an initiative statute similar to those passed in other states. This limited ballot access of all legislators and U.S. representatives to eight consecutive years and U.S. senators to twelve consecutive years. Initiative laws, unlike initiative amendments, can bypass the Con-Con process and be placed directly on the ballot. To obtain their goal LIMITS collected 110,000 signatures.

Indeed, on Election Day, November 8, 1994, the voters approved the ballot access initiative. But by 1995 the law was invalidated, due to the Supreme Court ruling. Since then LIMITS has been fighting its cause in the courts with no great success. Motions initiated by the movement are being denied on regular basis.

Is the story of Massachusetts a sign of things to come? Will the destiny of the movement be similar to that of the ERA, when more states will be approached to recruit their support for a constitutional amendment? These and many other questions are, to a large degree, still open. We turn next to the examination of the costs and benefits associated with the effects of term limits at the states level and in general.

Chapter Five

Costs and Benefits of Term Limits

[Term limits on congressional service would]
help cure senility and seniority—both terrible
legislative diseases.
—Harry S. Truman

Term limits are already imposed legally and practically on the period of service of many American executives and legislators. Not only are the president's terms of service limited to only two periods of four years, similarly de facto limitations are imposed on the terms of his administration officials. Also as was shown in the previous chapter, many governors, mayors, and other elected officials, in addition to city and state legislators in various places, may not serve more than a designated period of time. This period is usually no longer than twelve years.

A cynical but not necessarily wrong view of politics would attribute the rationale underlining these restrictions to the outsiders' ambition to also enter into the political systems. Indeed, if incumbents and their staffs block the political system, then one effective way to penetrate it is to force them out by legal means. After all, it should not be forgotten that laws are accepted devices society invents to regulate real or potential conflicts that may evolve among its members. Just like "the right of way" directive, a traffic light or a policeman, helps regulate conflicts that may develop among drivers at various levels of intensity, so term limits settle political disputes among insiders and outsiders.

Because term limits are already a political reality in the various states and because they may spread over the years to others states as well as to the federal level, it is of some interest to examine what costs and benefits are associated with their broader implementation. For that purpose we have singled out three variables that dominate the ongoing controversy between the pro and con of term limits, regarding how it contributes to the management of American political life. The following examines their implications.

The first variable deals with the issue of experience or lack of it, which is associated with the consequences of replacing old veterans with new politicians. The second variable refers to the effects such replacement may have on efficiency and the effectiveness of the elected officers' work. The third analyzes the effect of the time variable on the selection process of representatives. Of course, these three variables are not mutually exclusive. In fact they are so interrelated that at times they merely define a different way of looking at the same thing. But because such variations in people's perceptions lead to a different type of evaluation, it necessitates a different kind of analytical emphasis or point of departure (Nachmias 1981). They are therefore dealt with as if they are indeed independent of each other. In the real world of politics, however, they are not.

The following analysis of the three variables is not conclusive, of course. It supports the status quo in some cases and the proposed change in others. This chapter does not resolve the debate one way or another. It presents the rationale for some of the major elements included in the ongoing controversy.

Legislative Experience

One of the most common arguments against term limits relates to the contribution of personal experience to the work of the legislator, and hence to the public interest. In essence it is argued that if legislators' terms were limited, then the executive branch would have the upper hand in the power struggle that prevails in the political arena. This would violate the notion of "checks and balances" that should exist between the three branches of government. Of course, the reference here is not to the executive whose terms are limited either de facto or de jura; rather, it is directed to the bureaucracy. Indeed, the distinction between the bureaucracy and the executive branch is important, even if these two entities are often referred to as a single category.

The bureaucracy is a permanent body employing people for a lifetime career, while the executive branch is not. The term of service of the executive branch is limited and is dependent, more or less, on the term of the chief executive, such as the president, the governor, or the mayor. This enables bureaucrats to develop much experience in handling both their designated tasks and the members of the other branches, including the executive one. In fact, based on the accumulative experience, bureaucrats develop an organizational memory far exceeding those developed by the other branches (with the exception, of course, of the upper levels of the judiciary branch). Bureaucrats become an interest group, or a power group, if one uses another interpretation (Appleby 1949); and because they have the proper tools, they usually get their way in spite of the natural opposition coming from elected officials. Max Weber (1958), the German scholar whose ideal model of 'bureaucracy' is most often cited as a prescription for an efficient method of managing public affairs, writes on this matter:

> Under normal conditions, the power position of full-developed bureaucracy is always overpowering. The "political" master finds himself in a position of the "dilettante" who stand opposite the "expert" facing the trained official who stands within the management and administration. (232)

Indeed, in Great Britain, where the bureaucracy (i.e., civil service) is the constant and the politicians are the variable, the prevailing tension between them became part of a folk culture that was translated into a successful 1980s television serial. In that program, "Yes Prime Minister," the elected prime minister (who in his early role was just a minister) had to continuously be creative and invent ways to bypass the automatic opposition of his chief bureaucrat, who endlessly tried to tackle any innovation or change in the normal inertia of government's activities (Lynn and Jay 1986).

The bureaucrats have the power because they need not stand the frequent test of public approval through elections; thus they stay longer in the system. They have some other advantages, two of which seem to be most important: control over information and a practical veto power. The bureaucrats have wide-scope knowledge and sophisticated tools to accumulate and process information. Executives and legislators do not have such tools, so they must rely on the information they obtain from the bureaucrats for their decisions. In doing so, they run the risk of incorporating the preferences and the interests of the bureaucrats, and not of their constituencies, into the formulation of their policies. A bold illustration of this type of unequal relationship exists between the military forces and the elected officials. The latter must make decisions, sometimes even declare wars, on the basis of information supplied by the former. Clearly, if the former hold pro-war preferences it would be rather difficult for the latter, who are responsible and accountable for public safety, not to follow suit. Gradually, "the military-industrial complex," as the coalition of bureaucrats and industry people are often called, begin dominating the perception of elected policymakers regarding security issues (Mintz 1985).

To protect themselves against such an interest-guided biased view of reality, elected officials have to develop checking devices, including the building of additional institutions to investigate the operation of the bureaucracy (e.g., state comptroller). Likewise, they rely heavily on the revealing capacity of the press, which consequently becomes an essential protective mechanism of any working democracy. Wildavsky (1974) reports on the methods used by the legislators to examine the validity of the budget, a document drafted by professional bureaucrats. Because it is presented in a line-item fashion, legislators choose to concentrate on one or some items, thus becoming experts in these areas. They consistently refuse to adopt any alteration in the structure of the budget, which could make it more rational by connecting ends to means, because they do not wish to forgo their specific powers of control.

Krehbiel (1991) provides the explanation for why this concentration occurs—why legislators tend to specialize over certain issues while ignoring others; why they become "champions over an issue" (Doron 1986). Accordingly, most legislators act in the context of uncertainty about the relationship between legislative solution and social problems. Furthermore, not only can they not define the causality between their decisions and the actual consequences, they are also unsure how their constituencies would react to them. Subsequently, they identify a subject area or an issue, and begin to accumulate specific information on it. In the process, information is translated into knowledge, and this helps reduce the uncertainty. They thus become experts, willing to trade their knowledge to others who become experts in other areas. This division of labor works for the benefit of all members of, say, a congressional committee; it is not necessarily compatible with the public interest.

When experts hold a monopolist position over knowledge, their preferences dictate the outcomes. They thus acquire a power position, and when "their" issue becomes publicly salient, they also gain the desired media exposure.

The other advantage bureaucrats have over elected short-term officials is what we call practical veto power. Elected officials may decide anything they wish, while bureaucrats are expected to implement these decisions. This is how the system is designed to work, and in many cases this is the law. But bureaucrats might decide to oppose these elected officials' decisions on ideological, professional, or even personal grounds. Any change may endanger their positions in the power arena, or it may introduce some elements over which they have no control. Hence, they often may do little things to prevent such initiatives from coming through. Climatic conditions, lack of budgets, mistakes in calculations, unrealistic time-tables for implementation, bugs in the design, and so on are all good excuses for not properly executing a decision taken by the elected policymakers.

Given this reality, the task of the elected officials is to supervise the bureaucrats so that their programs are executed in time for the benefit of the public. For it is an essential principle of democracy that they, in particular the legislators, serve as the true interpreters of the public interest, even though this notion is not clear and bureaucrats often believe otherwise (Redford 1958). Indeed, in this capacity many veteran politicians gain much experience in handling bureaucrats over the years, and from the point of view of their electorate, this fact constitutes great advantage for the community. Novices, on the other hand, need to spend time developing such handling skills and learning how to effectively control the administration.

So, to maintain the proper power balance in the polity, experienced politicians should be preferred over new ones because they reduce the ability of the administration to pursue programs that are not consistent with the short- or long-term wishes of the public. Are there other areas where veteran legislators are so clearly preferred over inexperienced ones? Note that in the above case, to minimize the apparent advantage, newcomers could hire the services of experienced professional staff. But then again, even in such cases, they run a similar risk of being captives in the hands of these professionals.

Personal experience gained while working in legislative bodies is considered one of the most important costs society has to pay, if society wishes to limit the terms of the representatives' service. Therefore, the nature of the ambiguity in determining areas where veterans are preferred over new ones should be clarified. We turn next to the analysis of the meaning of "experience" as it applies to the legislators' work. The notions of learning or experience curves assist the analysis.

Learning, Experience Curves, and Seniority

People learn and gain experience the more they do the same things over and over. When conditions are similar and people are asked to perform the same task, then they learn how to avoid mistakes, how to make efficient shortcuts, and how to reduce the costs of operations. This learning process continues until the performance of a new task is required, that is, until a new "cycle of operation" begins. This process is therefore a basic human condition. The degree at which an individual learns over time, the span of time that elapses from the beginning of the task until its completion—the shape of the cycle—could be described as a curve. A learning curve is a description of the rate at which an individual learns while performing a certain task repeatedly. When a new task is initiated, a new learning curve may be constructed to define the process. Various tasks are defined by different curves, depending on the propensity of learning for each of the given tasks. In a more complex task, say, involving some technological sophistication, learning rates may be smaller and slower than in a less technical area like riding a bicycle or cleaning a room. Different people may have different curves for the same tasks, of course.

Because organizations, like automobile factories or the U.S. Congress, are a conceptual categorization of an aggregation of people but are not the individuals in and of themselves, then they cannot learn in the sense described above. We therefore define the process of learning that takes place in them by experience curves. Like individually defined learning curves, group-related experience curves bring an overall reduction in the costs of operation to a given organization (Doron and On 1983). Experience curves are a way to aggregate, usually on the average, sets of individual learning curves. Experience curves are thus "the underlying natural characteristics of organized activity, just like a bellshaped curves is an accurate description of the normal random distribution of anything from human IQ to the size of tomatoes" (Hirschmann 1964:125). On the average, then, one can assess the rates of cost reductions for a given function and for a given industry or organization. Such assessment is important for the calculation of the level of investment needed for the construction of prospective products or services, and for assessing the expected returns. For example, it should make a great difference if in planning a new product (say, airplanes) calculations are based on a cycle of one hundred units or of one thousand units. The price of a unit to the consumer cannot be based merely on the costs associated with constructing the airplane's prototype. The price would be based, among other variables, on an average figure that is defined by the length of the cycle (i.e., the number of units included in it) and by rate of experience (i.e., the rate of cost reduction in making each additional unit in the cycle). Clearly then, pricing would yield greater profits the closer the unit's tag to the origin of the cycle, and the further the number of units sold to its end. This principle can be shown as follows, where the experience function is defined as a relationship between the number of the cycles and the costs of producing them:

$$C(N) = f\,C(1)x\,NB\,(-1 < B < 0)$$

Where: $C(N)$ is the cost of operation cycle N, $C(1)$ is the cost of the first cycle, N is the number of cycles in the process, and B is the coefficient of the experience rate.

Can one use this simple description to also understand advantages gained by veterans in the political arena? Certainly, in the area of electoral campaigning, veterans have an advantage over challenging newcomers. Perhaps the experience they gained in earlier campaigns should be added to the set of factors that so decisively contributed to their almost certain victory, which was presented in chapter 3. For in electoral campaigns, often the opposition exploits even the slightest of mistakes, including some marginal slip of tongue, to transform winners into losers. Experienced campaigners usually know how to avoid or manage mistakes (Doron 1996). Periodic electoral campaigns are indeed "cycles of operation." The veterans know how to distribute their efforts and resources between Washington and their states and between their capital and their voting districts (Fenno 1978). They also know how to talk and how to identify target populations, when to commit themselves and when to avoid the issues, whom to approach amongst certain people and groups for resources and whom to invite for endorsement. They need not have exact plans, nor need they be Machiavellian. Almost as a matter of second nature, they develop political intuition based on learning and internalization of past mistakes, and their accumulated experience helps to guide them through the campaign times.

Term limits would certainly put to waste all of this accumulated knowledge. It would perhaps reduce the personal welfare of certain individuals, forcing them to search for a different source of livelihood. It may also send to the job market all those individuals who were associated with the veterans' organization for some years. But this is merely an individual-level type of consequence with little or no relevancy to the welfare of the community of citizens. It is more important to examine what the advantages to the community would be by limiting the experience gained by the veterans' actual legislative work.

There are several identifiable operational cycles in legislative work. Prime among them is the bargaining, negotiation, and approval of national or state budgets. Because the budget must be approved as a binding act, a law, each year legislators must follow certain steps in order to see the process through (Wildavsky 1988). Novices would have to spend time and patience in an effort to learn the technicalities of the budgetary process; veterans would cut right through toward the important substance. Novices would have to follow the directives of the experienced politicians, sometimes at the costs of the welfare of their constituencies, or they may not enjoy their endorsements in future elections. Veterans are the heads of congressional committees; they are the planners and the strategists. Let's see why.

There is much to be said against the congressional seniority system as it operates at the national and state levels, and much has been said for and against it (Harrington and Tolman 1998). Its main disadvantage is the veteran's real blockage over the novices' routes of progress and to political influence. Talented freshmen and junior members of Congress work hard "on less important matters while waiting [quietly] to become seniors . . . [and] those individuals with more experience are likely to have more influence" (Ripley 1988:121). This is to say that political influence, obtained by, for example, becoming heads of important congressional committees, is, among other things, a function of the surviving capabilities of politicians in the electoral arena. It has very little to do with the quality and the substance of the performance of the politicians in the congressional arena. Barbara Hinckley recognized other consequences of the seniority system including the adverse effects on the congressional decision making process due to generational gaps, rural and conservative biases, non-competitive regions, and lack of outside party influence (1971:3).

Shepsle and Bonchek (1997) recognize the advantages of the seniority system but also its associated costs. They write:

> There are benefits and there are costs, however. Senior
> individuals may well be knowledgeable, familiar and
> experienced . . . but they also may be unenergetic, out of
> touch, even senile. Even when these liabilities do not appear,
> senior members may nevertheless be out of step with their
> committee and the parent chamber. (342)

However, the seniority system seems to produce at least two important political advantages: stability and predictability. Seniority system introduces a respectable measure of certainty to the work of the institution in which it exists. More often than not, one can be almost sure (and these include the executives and bureaucrats who deal with the legislators) that certain congressional members will return to their posts after the elections and continue the operation cycles that were briefly interrupted due to their campaigns. Veterans would continue to head committees, and experts in certain fields would continue to champion these fields of interests. Hence, attitudes of the non-elected officials should be different when they meet new faces after the election than in a situation when they meet the same faces. In the second event, postponement of a decision may not be a rational way to avoid its implementation.

And there is another explanation, more elegant, concerning the continual support for senior incumbents, even by those who favor term limits (Tabarrok 1994). This involves a prisoners' dilemma-type line of reasoning (Ordeshook 1986). It goes as follows: While all politicians can produce public goods that could be shared by everyone, voters elect seniors because it is rational: they have more power to produce pork that is beneficial for their own specific voters. But if all reason the same way, no one gets the pork, because seniority is hierarchical and relative. However, by not reelecting seniors, no pork would be produced and hence the voters would be worse off. On the other hand, politicians understand that regardless of their performance, the more senior they get, the more likely it is that they will be reelected. Also, politicians understand that only the production of pork and not of public goods will reward them politically. Since there is little threat to their post, they do little for the public either in terms of public goods production or in terms of pork production. This prisoner's dilemma game type of interaction, which produces suboptimal results, has some very strange consequences, some which were mentioned by their "names" in the preface to this book.

The reason for this strange democratic phenomenon of very old politicians serving in Congress for over thirty years, or alternatively having states and voting districts represented for very long periods (e.g., the Democratic South) by people who face no real opposition during election, could also be explained by rational reasoning. Voters know that the more senior a politician gets, the more influential he or she could be, and the more pork he can deliver. Hence, even if their politician is presently not senior enough in the congressional hierarchy, a repetitive election could bring him or her to that position of influence. Since voters do not know how voters in other states and other districts will vote, their best strategy is to keep voting for "their" candidate over and over again. If they stop and elect a new politician, they provide an advantage to representatives of other states and of other districts. This would work against their interests. Hence, by stopping voters' bidding against each other, term limits would reduce these self-interested incentives to ever making representatives senior.

Note also that it is rational for some states not to enforce term limitations upon their representatives. By using this mode of defection, these states' representatives would become seniors in a shorter time span. They would thus become more influential than term-limited politicians for the benefit of the people in their states.

Term limits break down operational cycles. It sends the negotiators (e.g., lobbyists, interest groups, and administrators) to a new bargaining table. Although the novices are not required to, they begin their legislative work from a de facto zero basis. In due time the effect of learning and experience will take place and they too will be able to improve the quality of the cycle. Moore and Steelman (1994) produced a conceptual simulation (i.e., a "what-if" type of analysis) in an attempt to assess the effect of term limits on congressional decisions. They found out that if only junior members of Congress had been voting, as would be the case if all members were term limited, many popular fiscal reforms would have been approved including balanced-budget amendment and a line-item veto for the president. They also found out that proposals for tax increases would have probably been defeated under term limits.

A similar operation was conducted by John Berthoud (1998), president of the National Taxpayers Union Foundation. For his analysis of the Senate vote on the proposed Balanced Budget Amendment (BBA), he made the following assumptions: first, all Republican senators (fifty-five) would support the BBA, as they actually did. Second, of the forty-five Democrats, had term limits been enacted, the BBA would receive fourteen instead of the eleven it actually did. This is because Democratic senators who have been in the chamber for less than two years were twice as likely to vote for the BBA as more senior members. Consequently, he concluded, that had term limits been in place, the Senate would have supported the BBA with two votes to spare. Indeed, with term limits the two-third majority for the BBA would have been obtained.

Disregarding the scientific validity of these two analytical operations, the similar conclusions arrived at is of some interest because they point to the learning effect that presumably takes place in Congress. It shows in the first analysis that the more time a person spends in government, the less fiscally restrained he or she becomes. And in the second case, that time spent in Congress does not affect Republicans, only Democrats. What can one make of this? That a Democrat is less ideologically committed than a Republican? After years of service, a Democratic congressman understands the difficulties involved in an attempt to run an effective government, one that is sensitive to the demands of the people. He or she also understands that to solve problems one needs resources— that is, more taxes, even though they may disagree ideologically on the question of which problems should be solved first. Perhaps the above findings, which point to the conservative effect that might be generated by term limits, constitute some ground for a liberal-Democratic opposition to such limitations.

But, of course, in Congress and in state legislatures' bodies there is more than routine in legislative work. Some aspects of political work are reactive, responsive, creative, manipulative, intuitive, and visionary, all attributes that are necessarily enriched by long stays in institutions or by being involved in a particular legislative cycle.

Consider the following manipulative beauty of how to defeat an idea while supporting it. The method used could be labeled the "Tactics of the Exact." As reported by Holman (1997) in a debate in the U.S. House of Representatives over the issue of introducing an amendment to limit the terms of congressmen, Rep. Asa Hutchinson (R-Arkansas) said:

> The voters of Arkansas have specifically detailed the constitutional amendment that they want. And out of respect for the people of Arkansas, I'm offering this substitute amendment. And out of respect for them, I will also vote against any version that does not comply with the Arkansas language; therefore, I will vote against Mr. McCollum's bill not because I'm opposed to term limits but because this

particular resolution does not comply with the term limit
instructions approved by the voters and the people of
Arkansas.

These manipulative attributes may be acquired outside of the political
arena, of course, or at its lower levels. Indeed, in bad times in the nation
or the community, when fresh ideas are required, these attributes become
more important than the attributes people come to expect from the senior
politicians. It is possible, or at least plausible, that in bad times the
solution to the problem could come only from outsiders. A search for a
leader outside of a conventional political system in bad times is a known
phenomenon. Charles De Gaulle of France in the 1960s and, to some
degree, post-Watergate Jimmy Carter are two illustrations of this
collective instinct. Term limits can induce the introduction of creative
outsiders. However, the newly elected ones provide no assurance that
their performance would be better than that of the experienced politicians
they replaced.

The reason for the absence of such an assurance is quite simple.
Politics is not a profession in the conventional sense, even though many
would refer to veteran politicians as professionals. It is an occupation
that requires no special skills, no special education or training. A person
who wishes to become a politician need only meet the requirements
specified by the Constitution, and these are very minimal, general, and
inclusive. If his or her initial bid for an elective post is successful, then
the chances are that a lifetime occupation rewarded by respectable pay is
secured. Such a person need not invest his or her early adult years, as
most professionals do, in training programs or in higher learning
institutions designed for prospective politicians. Such institutions do not
exist in democratic systems. Departments of government or of political
science in various universities are not training grounds for future
politicians; they are, at best, places where young people may learn about
those politicians. And although an individual may personally benefit
from acquiring legal skills, being a lawyer is not a precondition for an
effective politician. Understanding the legal framework may make his or
her legislative work more beneficial to the community, but it may not.
Voters, on their part, may or may not take such candidates' skills into
their consideration at the time of decision. However, the individual in the
legal profession may have the flexibility (e.g., time and access) to both
campaign and provide a place to return to after a political loss.
Consequently, as shown in chapter 4 while the percentage of lawyers in

American legislative bodies decreased over the last three decades, it is still usually higher than that of other professions.

Because there are no institutions to train politicians and it is unclear what type of skills or knowledge such persons should be equipped with, we have no early capacity to tell whose job performance will meet our expectations. We have some basis with regard to future generals, artists, carpenters, or engineers, but not politicians. One can trace the career pattern of soldiers and tell if they are made of the stuff that characterizes generals. One can also examine the quality of artists' early work, or the ideas young engineers produce to solve complex problems, in order to determine the likelihood that they will do well in the future. One cannot, however, do the same thing with politicians. They are elected and then learn and gain experience on the job, paid by the public. They quickly learn how to perpetuate their situation and how to get reelected. They also learn how to please enough people so that they will continue to support their position. While term limits affect this ability, it is not clear if it helps select better politician or just different ones.

Effectiveness vs. Efficiency

Another common argument against legislative term limits and in support of the status quo puts much emphasis on the contribution of experienced politicians to both the efficient workings of the government and its effectiveness in obtaining its policy goals. Efficiency and effectiveness are two different concepts that are often used interchangeably. Efficiency is essentially an economic term, or at least its underlying rationale has been considered as such. It relates investments to products and inputs to outputs. It seeks to define the best ratio between costs and benefits. To be more efficient means that one either reduces costs while keeping benefits constant, or alternatively, expands benefits while keeping the costs constant. In the first case efficiency is associated with saving and in the second it signifies growth and production.

An efficient state would be one where no further changes could be made to either decrease costs or increase benefits. Therefore, this could also be captured by the notion of Pareto Optimality. Pareto Optimality can be defined in many ways; one acceptable way is as a state in which one can benefit (i.e., increase personal utility) only at the expense of others (Arrow 1974). That is, in an efficient economy one can improve his or her own position or welfare only by reducing the others' welfare.

Changes made at the Pareto frontiers, therefore, take the shape of zero-sum. Hence in order for all to gain, the economic frontiers must first be expanded.

Note that while efficiency is a highly valued condition in the private market because of its relationship to lower wastes and higher profits, it is not and ought not to be perceived as such in the public sector. It is a concept whose normative content may be quite problematic, to say the least. The concept of economic efficiency, which dominates the thinking of market-oriented conservative policy makers, may oppose other values important to societies. One such value may be, for example, social justice. Efficiency does not take into consideration the effects the uneven distribution of wealth has on the functioning of the social network. Society may be perfectly efficient but quite disgusting from a normative point of view (Sen 1970). Indeed, repressive regimes are often quite economically efficient, at least in the short run, but completely intolerable from the perspective of humanist values. Many historical examples illustrate this point. It might be sufficient to mention the acceptance of a massive violation of all human rights by the pre-World War II German society and its later submission to the destruction of others' and of their own civilization by a Nazi regime that promised, among other things, efficiency in utilization of national resources. The German highways ("autobans") are, indeed, the best in Europe.

Effectiveness is another matter. It relates to the ability of individuals or groups to obtain their designated goals. And this may or may not be consistent with the notion of efficiency. For example, it is quite possible to speed up the "slow windmills of Justice" if we are willing to take the chance that some innocent individuals will be punished. In does not make economic sense to keep dozens of people on death row, letting them appeal and re-appeal their cases for many years. The large amounts of public resources committed to this purpose could be directed to areas where they might yield greater benefits for society and could even effect a reduction in the level of crimes. However, this is not a serious option for a just society. Most democratic societies invest in a long, careful, and highly loaded opportunity-costs process to try to minimize the random possibility that innocent citizens would be penalized due to occasional failures of the legal system.

To be effective, individuals and organizations need to know how to utilize available personal, internal, and external resources (Yuchtman and Seashore 1967, Goodman and Pennings 1977). If a legislator is sent to represent the interests of a given region, then he is expected to deliver both favorable legislation and policies. To do that, this person should make the right personal connections, build a supportive coalition for a given decision, bargain, negotiate, trade votes, and do whatever is necessary to obtain the proper conditions for the region.

Given the above-presented understanding of these two terms, it is time to ask how term limits affect both notions of efficiency and effectiveness. For that matter, assume that a representative is sincere and therefore he or she would perform his or her task with the same level of commitment in the first and the last stages of his or her term. Note, however, that this assumption does not stand the test of backward-induction, whereby the same logic that led to a certain level of performance at the nth stage applied also to the first one (Shepsle and Bonchek 1997:144). If so, then, the more time one spends in office the more efficient he or she becomes, providing that his or her talents are not merely involving reelection skills. This is because with knowledge, learning, and experience, the personal cost of performance devoted to the welfare of the community becomes lower over time, and hence higher quality policies could become available. This is, more or less, one of the central points made by the opponents of term limits. Of course, if one relaxes the assumption of "the same level of commitment" the inference would, *ceteris paribus*, be different. Thus, it is quite possible that a person's commitment to his task would be lower after, say, five six-year terms, and hence the advantage gained by longer stays in terms of efficiency in deliverance over the potential delivery of new politicians diminishes. The inference, then, is that one cannot generalize on the quality of the legislators' performance without observing it on a case-by-case basis. Records presented at election time may not provide sufficient information on this matter.

Would a longer stay in office make the legislator more effective than a shorter stay? Indeed, the answer should be affirmative if we again use the "similar commitment" assumption. When this assumption is relaxed, we again obtain inconclusive inferences regarding effectiveness. Therefore, since we are not clearly convinced which is a better method to mange public life—with or without term limits—we would rather stay with the certainty provided by the status quo, even if it turns out to be somewhat costly. Note, however, that to arrive at the above inference, our treatment of the concept of effectiveness has been similar in spirit to that which dealt with efficiency. That is, both were viewed from a public policy perspective and the welfare of the community. But effectiveness, as noted above, stresses the achievement of other societal or democratic values as well. Subsequently we now move to ask how term limits or a lack thereof affects the value of democratic participation.

Consider two simple situations. The first involves shareholders in an economic company, the second a shareholder in a polity (i.e. citizen). Both are asked to vote under similar structural conditions. Both are members of the minority group, which together hold 50 percent minus one share. According to both company and polity constitutions, the majority of the shareholders have the right to decide on all relevant matters. In fact, while the majorities hold only one share out of thousands of the shares held by the opposition, they control 100 percent of the power to make all forms of decisions. And under the right established by the respective constitutions, they use this power. In these situations, under what conditions would the minority of shareholders come to vote? Because their votes do not affect the outcomes, they would come to vote only if they think that voting is an important act in and of itself, or when they believe that somehow they will be able to obtain a majority. If not, then they would stay at home. They would presumably stay idle until dissatisfaction with the decisions of the majority motivated them to act in order to protect their assets. In the economic case these assets are their profits; in the political case it is the quality of their democracy.

Term limits seem to be conducive to assuring that the polity would be an effective participatory democracy; that is, that more and more people should get involved in the voting process and be elected. This means that the more people believe that active participation matters, the more people would participate. This is, in essence, the logic underlying Rational Expectations Theory (Sargent and Wallace 1976; Taylor 1983). Otherwise, the investments society makes to override "free rider" problems, to construct a cohesive stable society out of utility-maximizing independent rational individuals, would be in vain (Kook 1992). Participation is an important value that should be obtained by an effective democracy. Therefore, a clear case could be made for term limits from a "collective action" (Olson 1965) and effectiveness point of view.

The Time Factor

It is almost banal to analyze the effects of the time factor when term limits is itself a time-defining variable. We do that because we wish to concentrate briefly on two interesting elements associated with the time dimension as it applies to term limits: cycles and synchronization.

Cycles

Several types of casual relationships are used to explain human behavior. While much of the causality in social or policy interactions can be explained in a straightforward linear manner (i.e., A causes B directly), there are some types of political relationships that assume a cyclical shape. These relationships are due to the nature of the time intervals that define them. For example, it is a well-known fact that the president acts differently on policy issues in his second term than in his first. During the first term he must take into consideration the effects of his policies on his reelection bid; during the second term he is relatively free from such calculation. This goal replacement has a noticeable effect on the relation of foreign nations with the American administration. As Quandt (1986; 1993) observed, in designing foreign policy the president must take into account the effects of the working of the American domestic political system, "especially the four years cycles of presidential elections." This is because the cycle imposes some regular patterns on the policymaking process that have little to do with the world outside but "a great deal to do with the way power is pursued and won through elections."

It also affects the nature of domestic public policy (Tuftee 1978). Thus, for example, because people tend to favor the incumbents when economic conditions are good, and the challenger when they are bad, and because they tend to have a short memory, decisions to expand the economy are often made one year before the election.

In fact, many restrictions imposed on the economy are lifted before the elections; taxes are reduced and even larger sums of money (e.g., welfare or pension checks) are transferred to the recipients, often timed exactly on election day (Tuftee 1978). On the other hand, decisions to limit economic expansion, to increase the level of taxes or to add new ones, are made as far away from Election Day as possible to minimize their political effects (Ben Porth 1975). Furthermore, as shown by Doron and Tamir (1983), even when the national (and in fact any election-sensitive) budget increases incrementally every year in all of its categories, election years determine which areas receive greater increments of appropriations. These tend to be the "social" areas where there is a direct impact on the recipient's welfare. Other areas responsible for the production of indivisible "public goods" (Steiner 1977), such as national security, and where individuals are not able to assess the direct contributions of government's expenditures on their own personal welfare, would receive proportionately smaller increments. After the elections this rule would be reversed.

Several studies have found macro cyclical effects that are correlated to the political developments in America. Hibbs (1977), for example, showed that unemployment tends to fall when Democrats occupy the White House and rises when a Republican president takes his turn. Mevorach (1987) explains this by the difference in the orientations of the two major parties toward interventionists' policies. Democrats intervene more than Republicans, who tend in general to mix less politics with economic choices. Therefore, Democratic governments are more distributive, so during their reigns unemployment levels are lower. Alesina and Rosental (1988) further refine this understanding of the cyclical relationship that exists between the economy and politics. They observed that since World War II there have been two political economy regularities. The first is that the party of the president always loses votes in the mid-term congressional election relative to its congressional vote in the previous elections. The second is that the Republican administration exhibits below average economic growth in the first half of each term, and Democratic administrations are associated with above average growth. It could be inferred, thus, that to counterbalance the president's policy, voters use the mid-term elections to strengthen the opposition in Congress.

Could term limits affect the nature of this electoral economic cycle? The answer to this question is yes. While term limits could change the nature of the cycle, it cannot eliminate it. While, as Theodore White wrote citing Richard Nixon: "I always thought this country can run itself domestically without a president . . ." (as cited in Marder 1974:132), most voters seem to make their electoral choices based on their assessment of the expected contribution of the candidate to their own economic welfare. The essence of the representative's economic philosophy and, consequently, how he or she is expected to vote on economic matters, are crucial elements in voters' choices. Rarely would a candidate promise to increase taxes; seldom would he or she fail to indicate that public expenditures should and could be prioritized differently. Usually this economic self-interested motivation of the voters is stronger than many of the other considerations they take into account when they make their choices. Studies show that these self-interested considerations are even more important than voters' sincere positions on term limits. Again and again it is found that while up to 80 percent of the voters in the various states support term limits, a majority of them continue to vote for the incumbents. Could not they simply vote for the challengers, thus implementing, in effect, the term limits idea?

This "bizarre" contradiction can easily be explained and has been partly explained above when we discussed the seniority system. It constitutes the known "collective action" problem. Like the prevailing citizens' orientation toward paying taxes, presumably they hold the same position with regard to term limits. We are all supportive of paying taxes because it is in our interest and our duty as citizens, and also because we recognize the benefits obtained by us from the consequences of public expenditures. We know that these expenditures were made possible by our taxes. However, we would avoid paying those taxes if we were asked to do so on a voluntary basis, because our incremental contribution to the overall expenditures is negligible. In any case, once the public good (e.g., security, law and order) is produced, no one could deny us from consuming it (Steiner 1977). So why pay?

The logic underlying voters' attitudes toward term limits seems to be similar. People may be sincerely against the prolonging of the terms of the politicians for more than two terms because they believe that imposed time caps are good for all. However, at the same time, they may support an incumbent who has served for more than two terms because they want him or her to continue affecting legislation in a direction that favors their own interests. Hence, there is no contradiction.

When the terms of the politicians are limited, then the electoral cycle specified above would take its effect during the first term. Would it also change its nature during the second and last period? How would a politician decide on economic policy matters, knowing that his or her public service is about to be over? Our answer to these and related questions is quite frankly: we simply do not know. A learned answer depends on the individual politician's future plans. If a person wants to step out of public life, then it may be true that free of electoral considerations, his or her decisions would emulate the kind of choices made by, say, a professional economist or judge. However, if he or she plans to continue in one or another phase of public work (e.g., party position, another elected office, consulting), then there are no grounds to expect that the cycles would disappear in the second term. The decisions undertaken during the last days of office would not be any different from those taken at the the last days of the first term.

Synchronization

The idea of term limits is based on the understanding that time affects behavior; that is, the longer the stay in office, the more likely it is that the politicians would produce a sub-optimal performance. To make sure that the mandate to represent the people is somehow linked to their actual or potential performance, democracies require periodic elections. The purpose of elections is therefore, among other things, not only to select representatives but also to reconfirm past selections. If enough selectors (i.e., citizens) express their approval, then those choices made in the past will continue to prevail in the present and in the future. Term limits proponents argue that somewhere in this process the ability of the voters to make the right choices has gotten distorted. The unusual advantage an incumbent gains in affecting the process of selection is merely a reflection of this distortion or of a selection bias. Term limits is a method that comes to assure that this distortion would not be carried over for too long. Opponents of term limits argue that voting is the best selection mechanism; that it should not be tampered with; and that term limits really limit voters' freedom of choice among alternative candidates. They recognize, of course, the unusual advantage incumbents have in the election, but they ignore the effect that such a candidacy has on the selection process.

Both sides of the debate ignore another important relationship, one that exists between the periods of voting and the making of public policy. It makes a great difference if elections are being held every year, every two years, every three years, and so on. Intuitively and based on our experience, we know that very little serious policy changes can be enacted during the short period of a year. What, then, is the optimal unit of time to initiate, design, adopt, implement, and evaluate an essential piece of public policymaking? What is the frame of time needed for a completion of a policy piece so that the politician can come to the voters and say: "I have promised, I have delivered, please evaluate my performance and reconfirm me?" To answer this question we need to know first what the policy piece is. For there are policy solutions to people's needs that take a long period of time to implement and obtain positive results (e.g., education, transportation), and those that provide short term remedies (e.g., lowering taxes, welfare transfers). Since we cannot design voting systems in accordance with the legislative and policy tasks required from the representatives, we arbitrarily and *a priori* fix these periods.

In the United States these periods are fixed in the U.S. Constitution and in the constitution of each state in the Union. For whatever rationale the Framers were using to determine the time that should elapse between elections, it must have reflected conditions that existed during the middle of the 18th century. These conditions include a significantly shorter life span of the representatives and policymakers, a pre-industrial and unsophisticated technological world, uneducated electorate, and a dominant *laissez-faire* ideology whereby government involvement in society is minimal and therefore little is expected from it. In addition, and of no little importance, politicians were serving on a more or less unpaid voluntary basis. Under such conditions, two years of service could be sufficient for a representative. Two years are not enough for a senator. Madison, in *The Federalist* No. 51, explains why: "All that need to be remarked is that a body which is to correct this infirmity ought itself to be free from it, and consequently ought to be less numerous. It ought moreover to possess great firmness, and consequently ought to hold its authority by a tenure of considerable duration." So the six-year term for senators is longer than the time interval allotted to the representatives and the president. In 1912, after some half a century of constitutional struggle, a senator's term of service, which was designed to add a "salutary check on the government . . . [and] double the security of the people" (*The Federalist* No. 51), was decided by the people with the adoption of the 17th Amendment to the Constitution.

Four time units are subsequently used to select the people who manage America's public space. Representatives are elected for two years, executives (president, governors, and mayors) for four, and senators for six; members of the administration stay until their retirement age. These unsynchronized periods of service for the different political functions may have a significant deteriorating effect on the quality of public policymaking, as we shall explain next.

Suppose that several alternative policy plans are proposed to solve a certain social problem. Each of these plans has a different benefits-costs ratio, or alternatively each yields a different positive net-benefit product (Mishan 1976). The first program, A, represents the best ratio; the last program, D, the worst. The first program proposes the most comprehensive solution to the problem. Following the logic of the sequential decision-making model proposed by Berton Klien (Doron 1986), it requires two years of study and testing to identify which one of two possible routes for a solution would be more promising, and four years of investments in constructing the necessary infrastructures.

Benefits would be produced following the program's sixth year. They would reach their peak after an additional period of six years. In contrast, program D requires a simple choice of doing something to solve the problem. This choice could be enacted within two years. The other two programs are of the intermediate kind. Program B would start to yield benefits after three years, and program C proposes two plans: one which yields positive results after three years and the other only after five years.

Given the different time horizons of the policymakers involved, what would be their likely choices of the plans specified above? Clearly, administrators would prefer plan A. It is the only one that provides the proper "professional" solution to the said social problem. They can initiate it and personally see it through until its completion. It is designed to minimize potential mistakes (i.e., two years of study), and to lower the prospected costs (i.e., choice between the two options is made on an educated basis). It is, however, the most politically insensitive of all the plans. Members of the target population would have to wait from six to twelve years until they could be rewarded by the program's benefits. In the meantime, other members of society would have to bear the present costs of investments. In contrast, program D is the most politically sensitive. Although it may not provide a good solution to the problem, its selection indicates to the public that the decision makers are highly responsive to the people's despair, so they act immediately to resolve matters. In two years the politicians may come to the voters, show a "no nonsense" record of performance, and ask for reaffirmation. Braybrook and Lindblom's "disjointed incrementalism" is the decision-making strategy which best describes this mode of policymakers' behavior (1963). Namely, to meet demands imposed on them by the public, the political decision makers who are uncertain and often ignorant of the consequences of their decisions would "muddle through" as Charles Lindblom (1987) labeled this mode of operation in 1959 (i.e., "The Science of Muddling Through"). Because reliable knowledge concerning social problems rarely exists, the decisions taken are usually only at the margin; something has to be changed to appease the people, and that is what is actually offered by plan D.

The logic underlying the choices for the B and C programs are also politically sensitive. They involve other categories of politicians who are affected by different time horizons. The executive would support the second program, B, if it can assure benefits to begin in the third year. If not, plan D would be selected, at least during the first term of office. During the second term, serious considerations would be given to program A-type proposals, those that yield benefits after two years, unless calculations of party continuity prevail, in which case the preference would shift to a support of plan C. Plan C is the usual choice of policymakers. It is not merely a reflection of a political lip-service, as is program D. It is a program to which a personal label could be attached, as opposed to program A. Relatively speaking, politicians who seek durable public credit, one that can be translated into political capital, would seriously look into program C.

But which one of the two options in program C is more likely to be supported by the sincere policymakers? Here again, the choice rule is somewhat simple: if the program assures that positive gains could be obtained within three years, it would get the vote; otherwise, the five-year plan would be adopted. The executive would find a supportive House for its "default" plan of two years and a supportive Senate for the three-year plan. In the second term of the executive, logic dictates that the five-year plan would be the more likely choice.

This analysis is, of course, a bold oversimplification of the complex reality of decision making. The picture gets blurry because of the one-third possible change of the Senate's composition every two years. To adopt a program, negotiations usually take place between the three political groups, having the administration in the background to supply information. These negotiations are aimed at finding some common ground; these grounds (called equilibrium by the economists) are the political compromises that all can live with. In this sense, politics serves as a synchronizing mechanism between decision-making groups who hold different time horizons. In any event, from the point of view of the public, the program that would finally be adopted would be sub-optimal. In times of crisis, the long-term plans would be adopted; in normal times, the short-term would be the likely candidates.

Could term limits produce a better synchronizing devise? Politicians' knowledge that this is their last term would move them, presumably, closer to the adoption of plan A, the program of the administrators. That is to say that essentially being able to hold an administrative job for a very long time or, alternatively, being unable to continue in the political post amounts to the same policy effect from the public point of view. Because of term limits, the decision maker gets free of political considerations, so he or she can choose policy programs that promise the highest positive yields to the public. Because not all members of each group are elected at the same time and because the times they end their service to the public do not overlap, necessary adjustments (i.e., political negotiations) would be required.

But there are several other reasons that suggest that term limits imposed on elected representatives may provide administrators some extra powers, in addition to the power advantage which was described earlier. Wilson (1982) describes three sources of bureaucratic power. First, bureaucracy grows so large that it becomes immune from popular control. Second, bureaucrats often function in private rather than public hands, making it difficult to supervise. Third, discretionary authority is vested in the hands of public agency so that the exercise of power is not responsive to the public good. Control over information is another very important method of exercising power. Niskanan (1971) understood this and modeled it in his Monopoly Bureau Theory. Accordingly, the more information controlled by the bureau and the less information provided to the elected politicians, the more control it exercises over them. Politicians would have to find other ways to accumulate knowledge and information.

With term limits, the politicians become less experienced and so need more information to function. Consequently they become more dependent on the suppliers of information. In America, like in most other democracies, senior public administration officials who directly interact with politicians usually have some twenty years of experience in the service. They are therefore in a better position to advance their program. Also the direct heads of the administrators are the members of the executive branch whose lengths of term are either four or eight years. Together with the experienced administrators, they could easily control the public agenda. This means that they have the capacity to propose plans and programs to the post-term limits inexperienced politicians and convince them to adopt them. Consequently, the nature of the work in the Congress and in state legislatures might change. It may assume the prevailing pattern in the European parliament: a very active government and a parliament that usually serves to approve the executive programs and policies. This was not the outcome intended by the Founding Fathers or the promoters of term limits.

So how can we handle the problem caused by unsynchronized decision-making apparatuses? One way is to define one set of term limits for all, including elected politicians, nominated executives, and permanent administrators. The other way is to extend the time interval for all types of politicians to, say, fifteen-year terms as suggested by

Hayek (1979). Because both ways seem to be impractical, there is no need to analyze them here.

The analysis in this chapter shows that under some circumstances, term limits could be an effective tool for improving the quality of public policymaking; under other circumstances, it would not change a thing. To complete the costs and benefits analysis of the term limits, brief reference should be made to two other conditions associated with this policy: instability and the effect of technology.

Political Instability

Instability is a cost factor directly associated with term limits. It relates not so much to the fact that veterans are forced to leave their posts to be substituted by inexperienced politicians, but to the fact that "open races" may change the composition of the American political space. The established relationships that exist between individual politicians and their parties at the national and state levels would necessarily be changed. So would the relationships between the politicians and the public. Representatives of new groups may enter the arena, and it is not clear which of the two larger parties would benefit more; perhaps the greater benefactor would be the initiators of a third or a fourth party. All of this means that it would become increasingly difficult to predict future political developments when "open seats" become the norm.

Analysts would encounter difficulties in the prediction of political outcomes caused by unstable results, even if the policy of term limits was erased from the legal books in every state. This is because once the genie is out of the bottle, it is difficult to ignore its effects. Voters would become sensitive to the length of time each of the candidates served in office and would partly steer their choices in accordance with this information.

The Effects of Technology

While new technologies also introduce some measure of instability and difficulties in predictability, one can easily place them among the benefit factors of term limits. The reference is mainly to exploding new information technologies: fast computers, sophisticated means of communication, and the Internet. While this is not the place to explain the meaning and the effects of these developments on our political lives, what becomes clear is that adjustments must be made in order to obtain reasonable performances.

The new electronic technology offers high-speed processing capabilities, larger scope of data, and greater possibility of interaction among more people. It makes the time intervals of the past shorter and shorter, and so requires different people to handle the effects of these changes. Most senior politicians are unfamiliar with these technologies. Even within the framework of term limits, as shown in chapter 4, the time allocated to politicians becomes much too long. The reality of the so-called information age requires constant readjustments of knowledge and skills. Only term limits could assure that the proper young people will be able to tackle those changes for the welfare of society.

Chapter Six

Term Limits in Michigan

In 1992, voters in Michigan approved an amendment to the state constitution limiting terms for their state legislators. As was the case with several other states, the term limits measure in Michigan was approved by a large margin—in this case, 59 percent. The year 1992 was arguably when the nationwide term limits movement reached the summit of its popularity and efficacy. Twenty-one states, including Michigan (and excluding Utah; see chapter 4), had term limits initiatives approved by the voters. The average vote in favor of term limits was about 65 percent (Ferry 1994).

Michigan, then, was part of this nationwide trend toward term limits; however, one cannot fully explain how term limits became popular in Michigan merely by recognizing the national movement led by such groups as U.S. Term Limits and Americans for Term Limits. National interest groups no doubt played a significant role in campaigning for the issue in several states, perhaps even spearheading the effort, but each state has its own population, government, economy, and political environment. If term limits initiatives were passed in a state, that means there was something about term limits that the voters there found attractive. What follows is a brief description of Michigan—its politics, population, economy, and history. This brief examination is necessary to understand why term limits were passed and what effects they might have.

Political Background

By virtually any criteria imaginable, Michigan qualifies as one of the largest states in America. In terms of population, Michigan ranks as the eighth largest state, with more than nine million residents in the 1990s. Its economy is the ninth largest among the states with a per capita personal income that also ranks highly among the states, at nineteenth. Michigan is also one of only nine states with full-time, professional, large-staffed, highly paid legislators (State Legislatures 1994). This last statistic is critical because of the nine states with full-time legislators, only Michigan, Florida, California, and Ohio have enacted term limits for its legislators (Gray and Jacob 1994).

Despite having one of the few professionalized state legislatures in the country, Michigan has always depended on the executive branch for policy leadership (Browne and VerBurg 1996). Due to its staffing, professionalism, and the resources available, the Michigan legislature has the capacity for strong policy formation and analysis, but usually it is the governor who initiates major policy proposals. This legislative dependence on the executive branch goes further in Michigan than the mere assumption that exists in most states that the governor should be the chief legislator; in Michigan, the governor must not only introduce proposals, but he must also encourage legislators to act throughout the policy process. Browne and VerBurg believe that the professionalism of the Michigan legislature is the cause of its lack of initiative in many policy areas. Accordingly, professionalism in the Michigan legislature has made lawmakers more attentive to the diverse needs and interests of the state and also their constituents. As a result, they are more cautious, more willing to let the governor take the initiative on policy proposals, and less willing to assume the risks associated with statewide, controversial issues. The notion seems counterintuitive, but it is provocative. One of the reasons for the movement to professionalize the state legislature in the 1960s and 1970s was to make them less dependent on the executive branch for policy leadership. Browne and VerBurg contend that it has done the opposite, at least in Michigan.

Michigan is not a state that one can easily identify with one political party or one particular ideology, the way that New Hampshire is identified with the Republican party and conservatism, or the way Hawaii is identified with the Democratic party and liberalism. Politics in Michigan has been very competitive, at least since 1948, when a Democratic coalition emerged at the end of World War II. For the past fifty years, no party or ideology can be said to have been dominant.

Virginia Gray and Herbert Jacob devised an index to determine the level of competition between the political parties for state governmental control. For the period of 1988-1994, two different aspects of competition were included in the analysis: inter-party competition for government control and electoral competition. Michigan ranked quite highly among the states, at nineteenth (Gray and Jacob 1996). Even on the national level, Michigan is competitive. A majority of Michigan voters in 1980 and 1984 voted for Ronald Reagan for president, and in 1988 a majority voted for George Herbert Walker Bush; both were Republicans, of course. In 1992 and 1996, the Republican presidential nominee did not receive even close to a majority. In Michigan, partisan competition has been the norm for many years in electoral competition and intra-governmental control.

The term limits movement in Michigan began a full decade before the issue appeared on a referendum ballot. Far from being swept up in a nationwide movement that originated in California or Oklahoma (two of the first states to pass term limit laws), Michigan was one of the first states where the issue of term limits for state and federal legislators was seriously discussed. In Michigan, petitions were circulated to get what its supporters thought was the proper amount of attention directed to the issue, and sincere efforts to prevail upon the people and legislature to consider the passage of term limits laws were undertaken.

During the early 1980s, a nationwide recession had a particularly severe impact on Michigan. Unemployment was high, and automobile manufacturing was down. Dissatisfaction with the state and federal political system was at its highest level. If government is not the savior than it must be the villain, the cause for much of the prevailing social despair. It is because the wrong people are in the government for such a long time. Consequently, it was in the midst of this recession that Taxpayers United for Term Limits was formed. A petition was circulated in 1980-81 to put the issue of term limits for congressman and state legislators on the ballot. Close to 200,000 signatures were obtained, but it was not enough.

The early 1980s were a bitterly partisan time in Michigan politics. The poor economy no doubt contributed to the increasing combativeness between Republicans and Democrats. Debate on how to handle the recession grew more and more ideological. Republicans such as gubernatorial nominee Richard Headlee called for a reduction in state services, lower taxes, and a "business" approach to the budget, while Democrats wanted to increase aid to the unemployed and provide more state services to bolster the economy. Debates on term limits seem to emerge and flourish during politically divisive times. Term limits, despite historically receiving support from both major political parties, could indeed become a very ideological issue; and ideology often becomes a deciding factor in politics when bipartisanship and compromise are unlikely. Ideology could be understood as a close system of questions and answers, just like religion. And hence, in times of personal crisis, people tend to look for external answers to their problems. The concept of term limits provided a partial answer. It directed a finger toward the source of the problem: the political system. It also specified the method by which one could resolve matters: show the politicians the way out of their office. Expressing a desire for term limits on lawmakers may be symbolic of the frustration many have with a seemingly polarized, and therefore inert, political process. With this in mind, the formation of Taxpayers United for Term Limits comes as no surprise when one realizes the divisive state of Michigan politics at the time.

Despite failing initially to achieve the goal of putting term limits on the ballot, Taxpayers United for Term Limits tried again in 1988 but once more fell short of the necessary number of signatures needed in a petition drive to force the issue to a vote of the people. It was around this time, however, that term limits began making headlines as a national issue, with more and more people around the country becoming interested in limiting terms for both federal and state legislators. By the early 1990s, Taxpayers United for Term Limits would get some welcome help in achieving its goals.

The year 1990 witnessed the surprise election of John Engler to the governorship. The race was very close, representing the divisive combativeness in Michigan politics at the time. Democrats retained control of the state house, Republicans the state senate. In this environment, the term limits movement in Michigan became its most efficacious. Taxpayers United for Term Limits, based in Saginaw, was joined by the Taxpayers Association of Michigan, based in western Michigan. Draft amendments to the Michigan constitution were written; more petitions were circulated. Finally, in 1991, the national group

Citizens for Congressional Reform led a petition drive, culminating in the numbers of signatures needed to put term limits issue on the ballot for 1992.

The proposed term limits amendment to the Michigan constitution was based on the 22nd Amendment to the U.S. Constitution, which limited terms for the president. Pat Anderson, drafter of the amendment, attempted to make the amendment somewhat invulnerable to legal attacks or at least word it in such a way that the constitutionality of the amendment was secure. To do this, he made a crucial distinction between federal and state legislators. The term limits movement in Michigan, as well as in other states, knew of the possibility that the courts would eventually invalidate any alterations to the qualifications for congressional membership as enumerated in the U.S. Constitution. Therefore, many of the term limits laws and amendments were drafted keeping federal and state legislators a safe distance apart. This way the courts could invalidate a part of the amendment as unconstitutional (limits for the congressional delegation) while another part could be saved from invalidation (limits for state legislators). This is what would eventually transpire in the important and controversial Thornton case, to which chapter 2 is devoted (Interview, Pat Anderson, March 1999).

The Campaign for Term Limits

The campaign to put term limits on the ballot was intelligently waged by the issue's supporters. Western Michigan was a key geographic region. Glenn Steil, an important local businessman and the chairman of the Kent County Republican Party, was an enthusiastic supporter of the term limits cause, especially for federal legislators. His efforts were instrumental in obtaining the necessary number of signatures for inclusion on the ballot. The western side of the state in general was highly supportive of the issue—70 percent approved of term limits. Securing such a sizable support in this region of the state was crucial to the campaign's success since Michigan's largest urban area, the city of Detroit and Wayne County, did not have great enthusiasm for term limits.

The proposed amendment would appear on the 1992 ballot as Proposal B. The campaign over the issue was bitter and divisive, like so much of Michigan politics at the time. Supporters of the amendment, wanting to avoid being accused of partisan political machinations, attacked the "in crowd" of Lansing, legislators who had, in their opinion, overstayed their welcome. They were careful not to focus only on Democratic or Republican legislators (Interview, Pat Anderson, March 1999). Opponents of the term limits movement in Michigan, however, such as former speaker of the state house Lewis Dodak, maintain that the issue has always been purely political, as opposed to ideological. Namely, that many Republicans pushed for term limits solely so the Democratic majority in the state legislature could be defeated.

During the summer of 1992, U.S. Term Limits, a nationally based interest group, held a strategy session in Denver for all states with term limits laws on the ballot. The session included strategies for polling, defending the issue, attacking the opposition, and gathering support. This helped to provide cohesiveness to the individual efforts in the many states where the issue was on the ballot.

The opposition to term limits in Michigan was formidable. As is the case with many political issues, those arguing for some kind of change were more devoted and enthusiastic in their cause than those attempting to prevent the change. In Michigan, few politicians spoke out against the issue; term limits support among the voters was very strong, and many thought that merely voicing opposition to term limits, let alone actively campaigning against them, would hurt them politically. Nevertheless, intense opposition to term limits did exist. Several large companies in Michigan, including Edison, Upjohn, General Motors, Ford, and several labor unions, contributed resources to the fight against term limits.

Most politicians nominally supported the issue, but few actively campaigned for it. Governor John Engler is a good example. Though he lent his name to the pro-term limits movement, he did not once speak publicly about the issue. Engler's popularity at the time was tenuous, and he did not want to get directly involved with such a divisive, though very popular, issue.

In July of 1992, a formal committee for term limits in Michigan was created, with Steil and Richard Headlee (who had led the tax movement in the 1970s) as the co-chairs. The committee hired Steve Mitchell as executive director. Mitchell had previous experience working for a term limits campaign in Washington. This would prove to be an invaluable asset for the term limits committee in Michigan, as Mitchell was able to correctly gauge how the opposition would campaign against term limits.

Support for term limits among Michigan voters did not come solely from those identifying themselves as "Democratic," "Republican," or "neither." In fact, support came strongly from all kinds of voters. Two-thirds of Republican voters supported the issue, about half of Democratic voters, and, as expected, three-quarters of those who voted for independent presidential candidate Ross Perot, himself a supporter of term limits.

Those opposing term limits in Michigan, though strident in their opposition, were disorganized. Clearly they were at a disadvantage. Most public figures, even if they secretly opposed term limits, were unwilling to challenge a movement which was enormously popular throughout the state and the nation, and whose goals it seemed futile to try to block. As Daniel Loepp said, "We knew we were going to lose anyway" (Interview, March 10, Daniel Loepp).

Despite having virtually no public support from the state's political leader and continually trailing by a large margin in the public opinion polls, the opposition movement nonetheless was able to voice a strident opposition to term limits. An opposition group, Michigan Citizens against Term Limits, was formed in June of 1992. It was a coalition of groups that included the League of Woman Voters, Common Cause in Michigan, and the Michigan Municipal League. One of its primary campaign strategies, which was used more vigorously as election day neared, was to charge that the term limits movement was not a grass-roots effort led by ordinary citizens who were seeking to change government for the better, but rather a movement led by politically conservative special interest groups. Their evidence to support this claim was the origin of much of the funding for both the petition drive for Proposal B and its subsequent campaign. Citizens for Congressional Reform, a national interest group based in Washington D.C., had contributed more than $200,000 to Michigan's Campaign to Limit Politicians' Terms (CLPT). CLPT would eventually become the Say Yes to Proposal B campaign. But Michigan Citizens Against Term Limits (MCATL) viewed this as something more sinister than mere funding from a powerful interest group. According to MCATL, Citizens for Congressional Reform was a "dummy organization" created by two oil billionaires, David and Charles Koch, both libertarians, and representative of powerful politically conservative interests that were in fact controlling the term limits movement. Francis Parker, president of the Michigan League of Women Voters, said, "These are not people who, like Michigan voters, are sick of special interests. These are powerful special interests. The people of Michigan need to know what their agenda is so that they can evaluate it for themselves" (*Kalamazoo Gazette*, 15 Oct. 1992, A10). Kathy Pelleran, executive director for

Michigan Citizens against Term Limits, echoed those sentiments: "Our research shows that the supposedly "local" Michigan group has been bought and sold by Citizens for Congressional Reform, funded by the Koch brothers—they're calling the shots in Michigan. It's an elaborate, well-financed scheme, a complex web designed to hide the true affiliation from the Michigan voters—and that's fraud" (*Grosse Pointe News,* 29 Oct. 1992, A23).

The issue of campaign financing for term limits would eventually extend beyond the mere political quarreling so common with certain issues. MCATL would file a complaint with the Michigan Secretary of State's office, alleging that the out-of-state backers of term limits, which included the Koch brothers and Citizens for Congressional Reform, had not made specific disclosures of their contributions. Steve Mitchell called this a "diversionary tactic," claiming that MCATL was resorting to such measures out of desperation and that the term limits opponents could not win on the merits of the issue alone (*Grosse Pointe News,* 29 Oct. 1992, A23). Nothing came of this; the complaint was dismissed.

Spokesmen for the Say Yes to Proposal B campaign, including Steve Mitchell and Richard Headlee, while admitting the campaign had received substantial financial support from out of state, maintained nonetheless that the term limits movement was grassroots in nature, pointing to the simple fact that more than 400,000 signatures of Michigan residents were obtained during the petition drive. Also, the term limits campaign contended that it was MCATL, not the Say Yes to Proposal B campaign, that was the tool of special interests. MCATL had the backing of several large corporations and labor unions. Ford, General Motors, and United Auto Workers Union all backed the opposition and contributed significant amounts of funding to the effort.

The year 1992 was also marked in American politics by a strong "anti-Washington," "anti-insider," "anti-Congress" feeling. With the advantage of hindsight, it seems that term limits were inevitable and that the opposition could ultimately do nothing to stop the movement.

The term limits campaign in Michigan did not so much benefit passively from a poor economy, feelings of alienation, and a general anti-incumbency sentiment as it aggressively seized the advantage presented by the situation. In his outline for a campaign plan, Mitchell mentioned that one of the two major arguments for term limits was "corruption in the system" and how term limits was a remedy for ending the corruption. Bringing his experience with a failed attempt to pass term limits in the state of Washington, Mitchell warned about the possible use of "scare tactics" by the opposition (Memo on Campaign Plan, Steve Mitchell 1992). According to Mitchell, these were decisive in bringing about the defeat of term limits in Washington. Mitchell stressed the importance of not letting the public be taken in by what he called "the sky is falling!" campaign tactics (Memo on Campaign Plan, Steve Mitchell 1992).

In detailing the campaign strategy, Mitchell recognized three arguments for term limits for the "strongest emotional impact." First, term limits would guarantee that elected officials would devote more time to important issues instead of concentrating on reelection. Second, term limits would help end corruption in government. This was part of the overall anti-incumbency sentiment of 1992, due mostly to a struggling economy, that the term limits movement nationwide was able to capitalize on. Third, term limits would provide opportunities for more people to run for office, especially women and minorities. This last argument was important because it appealed to liberals and Democrats who would otherwise most likely oppose term limits (Memo on Campaign Plan, Steve Mitchell, 1992).

The Say Yes to Proposal B campaign modeled its overall strategy objectives on those of the successful campaign in Colorado two years earlier. The primary tactic used was an anti-incumbent argument that term limits reduced corruption, made legislators less likely to be the tools of special interests, and removed reelection as the main concerns for officeholders. Anti-incumbency sentiment, the calls for change, the need for new voices to be heard in the political system were, in fact, the driving political forces throughout the 1992 election, not just in Michigan but nationwide. Term limits rode the proverbial wave of the calls for change in 1992 and was a manifestation of an anger many felt with a poor economy and a political system that was seen as corrupt and uncaring. Nationally, Bill Clinton was able to defeat George Herbert Walker Bush for the presidency, running his campaign almost exclusively on economic issues. Independent candidate Ross Perot received 19 percent of the vote nationwide for the presidency, running on economic issues and proudly asserting his status as an "outsider." Overall, the successful term limits campaigns in Michigan and other states seized upon the desire to see something new in American politics, fear of a poor economy, and anger at perceived ineptitude, if not corruption, among the nation's politicians. Mitchell's outline for a campaign strategy very astutely hit upon the necessity of speaking directly to these sentiments; it would have been a futile exercise to attempt to create a fear and anger that did not already exist. The campaign strategy tried successfully to argue that term limits would be a cure for the many ills in American political life.

Extensive polling was done during the term limits campaign; Steve Mitchell has said that the entire campaign was poll-driven, as are much of the congressional and presidential campaigns. Polls were taken with increasing frequency throughout the campaign, with support for term limits always very strong. Mitchell has said that the strongest "selling point" for term limits was the belief that term limits would allow for more women and minorities to obtain seats in the legislature.

One of the most unfortunate results of the bitter term limits campaign in Michigan was that the long-term implications of term limits were never seriously considered. Neither the support nor the opposition ever brought into contention what ultimately would be the *effects* of term limits. From a policy perspective, neither side argued that term limits would result in better or worse laws being passed in a term-limited legislature. Instead, the campaigns both for and against the issue devoted themselves to more immediate political issues—removing entrenched incumbents, debating the legality and constitutionality of term limits, vague calls for change, etc. Only after the ballot measure was approved did many start seriously thinking about the policy implications of term limits.

Several key Michigan newspapers endorsed Proposal B. *The Detroit News, Lansing State Journal*, and the *Ann Arbor News* all urged the passage of term limits. Some newspapers, however, urged defeat of the proposal; they included the *Grand Rapids Press, The Detroit Free Press,* and the *Saginaw News.* Overall, it appears that newspapers' endorsements reflected the public opinion polls: Most supported term limits, but there was a strident and significant minority voicing opposition.

The measure passed rather easily. Despite having equal funding as the term limits movement, the opposition could not overcome a few disadvantages. One was the lack of nationwide interest group support. There was no counterpoint to U.S. Term Limits, Inc., Citizens for Congressional Reform, or Americans for Limited Terms that the opposition could look to for help during the campaign. Also, campaign spending by the opposition was poorly handled. With about two weeks before the election, when pollsters and politicians and campaign managers are usually preparing to mount a frenzied media blitz to support themselves and their issues, the opposition to term limits in

Michigan discovered that it had run out of money. This, according to Steve Mitchell, was their greatest mistake. It allowed term limits movements to take full advantage of those last two weeks with virtually no opponent. Such an amateurish error is indicative of the disorganized, unprofessional campaign the opposition waged. Through the will of the people and the opposition's own ineptitude, the term limits movement in Michigan achieved its goals.

The new amendment to the Michigan constitution limited state representatives to three consecutive terms of office (six years) and state Senators to two consecutive terms of office (eight years). Once the limit has been reached, the officeholder is banned for life from running for a seat in that chamber again. The disparity in the number of years a representative and senator may serve could lead to a shift in legislative power to the state Senate. Since a senator can serve up to eight years, as opposed to six for a representative, the senator will be able to accumulate more knowledge and expertise, so the argument goes. Only time will tell if this will indeed be the case.

Pro vs. Con

Philip Selznick (1966), in a classic study on the TVA (Tennessee Valley Authority) that was completed in 1949, introduces the concept of co-optation. Co-optation is defined as "the process of observing new elements into leadership or policy-determining structure of organization as a means of averting threats to its stability or existence" (Thompson and McEwen 1958:27). In his study Selznick showed how the Authority, which was formed during FDR's time to help the region and the American economy to get out of the Great Depression by transferring federal money for the building of dams in the Tennessee Valley, gradually shifted its goal. Indeed, here are the trained personnel, the organization, and the budgets, in addition to political support coming from the states that border the valley, so what makes more sense than to continue the promotion of public interests in other ways? The TVA adopted other goals, including political and social ones, and continued to operate even after most people had forgotten the initial reasons for its formation. In general, then, it can be said that public organizations once formed do not die; they just change the definition of their purposes (Downs 1957).

The term limits movement in Michigan, and for that matter in other states as well, did not put their weapons down after their initial success. The movement continued its operation in order to maintain two goals: protection of its achievements at the state level and expansion of the idea to the national level. This means a constant mobilization of activists and continuous fight over the control of the public agenda as expressed by the written and electronic media and against citizens' attempts to use the courts to reverse early decisions. Some examples from the activities that took place during one year, from late 1997 to late 1998, provide a partial picture of substance of the movement.

> **October 1997:** Detroit Court rejects opponent's request for preliminary injunction, sets schedule for case. Opponents campaign intensively against term limits in Dearborn.
> **December 1997:** Citizen intervenors (Al Schmidt, Patrick Anderson, and Taxpayers United for Term Limitation) file briefs on a Michigan case in the U.S. District Court in Detroit.
> **January 1998:** Patrick Anderson debates the opponent on public television.
> **February 1998:** The U.S. District Court rules that Michigan's term limit amendment is fully constitutional.
> **March 1998:** Three Wayne State University Law School professors whose earlier appeal to the Court against term limits failed, try again. This time they file suit in Wayne County Court and in the U.S. Court of Appeals for the Sixth Circuit.
> **April 1998:** Wayne County District Court dismisses the three professors' challenge.
> **May 1998:** The U.S. Court of Appeals for the Sixth Circuit rejects arguments that judges should overturn voters' will in favor of term limitation. Likewise, the Michigan Supreme Court upholds Michigan Term Limit law in a unanimous decision.
> **August 1998:** As a result of Term limits going into effect, the largest ever group of candidates run for office in the "open seat" races.

The Effects of Term Limits in Michigan

The term limits laws approved by Michigan voters in 1992 took effect in 1998 for state representatives. The impact was dramatic, as 64 out of 110 state representatives elected in 1998 were freshmen legislators. Of all the states in which term limits laws took effect in 1998, Michigan's turnover rate was the greatest.

It is interesting to see what, if any, effect legislative term limits will have on various cities, regions, and counties in Michigan. For instance, the metro Detroit area lost twenty-four members of the state House of Representatives due to term limits in 1998. Among the legislators forced out were House Speaker Curtis Hertel; Morris Hood, the chairman of the powerful House Appropriations Committee; and the heads of committees on Labor and Corrections. All are Democrats. Daniel Loeppa, former Chief of Staff for Hertel, now a lobbyist in Lansing, contends that the Detroit area and the Upper Peninsula will be the regions in Michigan most adversely affected. Loepp said in the aforementioned interview, "These people have traditionally served for a long time from these areas. That is how power is earned in the legislature—through seniority and experience. Term limits have taken these away."

Term limit supporters see the new laws as a vindication of the wishes of a strong majority who has wished for a citizen legislature more attentive to the public good. The opposing view sees the executive branch, the bureaucracy, and special interest groups as the big winners in the term limits competition. Due to rapid turnover, the executive branch will have a distinct advantage in knowledge and expertise and will be better able to push its agenda on an inexperienced lame-duck legislature. Those opposing term limits also see the opportunity for lobbyists to exercise more power in Lansing as they will be much better able to convince an inexperienced, unknowledgeable legislator on the wisdom of this or that political position.

Whatever the long term effects on the political power of the legislature vis-à-vis the executive branch and the bureaucracy, and whatever effects term limits may have on policymaking in Michigan, it is clear that they have already made a serious impact on state politics.

Chapter 7

Conclusion: What Difference Do Term Limits Make?

Legislative term limits will be adopted for the national level in the foreseeable future. Insofar as the essence of American polity will not radically be changed—the essentially two-party structure would not be transformed into a multi-party one—term limits will be enacted. This is not wishful thinking we dare to include in a scholarly account of the studied phenomenon. It is a prediction that is mostly, but not entirely, based on the analysis presented in this book. This is providing, of course, that the idea of term limits will continue to be placed high on the public agenda, as it was during the 1990s. However, since there are no reasons to expect that the idea will lose its saliency as a solution to political problems or ambitions, we dare to make the above prediction.

Term limits will prevail because there are few alternative options to obtain the effects that it promises. It is a way for ambitious outsiders, individuals who also want to play the political game, to change the prevailing partisan reality. It provides a sense of empowerment to the public, a sense of control over the politicians. It is a very simple form of electoral reform, simple enough for the voters to understand, and it is based on rejection, as opposed to approval, of the making of politicians. And, once internalized, it could serve as an effective tiebreaker between candidates. Of course, it will take time, perhaps a long time, until it will be legally—that is, constitutionally—adopted, but its practical effects will be recorded much earlier. Indeed, they are presumably already affecting the way some voters make their calculations regarding their political choices. All of these reasons have little to do with the normative underpinning or the intention of the Founding Fathers presented in this book.

Legislative term limits became an issue during the late 1980s because the performance of the American politicians had been publicly perceived as being of low quality. The "divided government" phenomenon analyzed with such a talent by Fiorina (1992), where the executive belongs to one side of the political map (i.e., the Republicans Reagan and George Herbert Walker Bush) and the Congress to another, is not uniquely an American situation. In the French presidential system and to some degree in minority governments that rule European parliamentary systems, quite often one political camp blocks the other side's initiatives, thus preventing government from providing effective policy solutions to mounting societal problems (Maor 1992; Laver and Schofield 1994). Political stalemates due to such mutual blockage must have deteriorating effects on the citizens. They presumably learn to rely less on the political system to provide solutions to their problems and more on themselves. The parallel emergence of the concept of "civil society" in the West and in other places, whose motto is self and communal reliance, is part of this effect (Seligman 1992; Norton 1995).

Another effect is, however, more relevant to the analysis presented in this book. Term limits is a form of organized political articulation of public "voice" against its politicians. In good times the public, or most groups included in society, are loyal to the rules of the game. In prolonged bad times that leave the public little hope for improvements, these groups may decide, to use Hirshman's vocabulary, to "exit" (1970). Political exits may take various forms: Indifference is one form; revolution or radical opposition to the prevailing status quo may be another (Gurr 1970). Voice is a message sent to the politicians during bad times telling them to clean up their act. If they do not respond according to expectations, changes might be enacted. The public might put restrictive conditions on the content of the mandate it delegates to its representatives. Term limits is this form of such restriction.

Admittedly, the message may be read and interpreted by politicians in various ways, and consequently so could their responses be the "voice" of the public. Some politicians may adjust their policy positions, making them more suitable to what is requested by the public. These populist-oriented policies may be confronted with policies that constitute their mirror image: liberal market-oriented positions that reinforce and legitimize the prevailing disappointment from government's ability to provide solutions (Riker 1982). American and British proponents of the latter approach to the "market of ideas" won the political power game decisively during the 1980s. But since then, there seems to have been some erosion in their dominance, at least in Western Europe.

Another possible response is a political realignment, a change in the composition of the political parties that traditionally represent the public. It happened in Canada, Japan, and other democracies during the early 1990s (Doron and Harris 2000). In general, voters' traditional loyalty to their parties seems to be fading somewhat in several European countries where they quite frequently shift their alliances from one election to the other (Zuckerman 1990). In addition, new issues (e.g. environment, personal accountability) and new faces seem to replace the traditional ones and the politicians who failed them. This gradual process of realignment has not happened in the United States yet. Except for the two time electoral bids of Ross Perot, whose third party was able to affect the outcomes of the presidential election (in 1992 and 1996) but not of the two-party structure, no major political change took place during these years.

Compared with his predecessors George Wallace and John Anderson, who were promoting a clearer ideological position than the ones advanced by the candidates of the two major parties, Perot seems to have a different kind of agenda. His political messages were essentially "anti-political." They articulated the voice of many citizens who were not as concerned with the direction their political system takes as with the way it operates. It is not surprising, therefore, to find out that term limits became a central political theme of Perot's supporters. Indeed, these supporters are usually the most devoted "term limiters," voters who choose the third political option to essentially terminate the term of the present politicians. And they want this outcome now, not in eight or twelve years. Their unsuccessful electoral bid is a result, among other things, of their inability to move about half of the American electorate from their form that Chester Barnard (1938) labeled as "indifference zone" to the active zone, to motivate the so-called non-voters to come to the voting booths on Election Day and express their political preferences.

From this perspective, it would not be difficult to argue that the American two-party system has been preserved for so long not because it is effective but because many of the Americans do not care for it. The non-voters, however, presumably seem not to believe that much can be done presently to change the situation. Some prominent political scientists, including Gabriel Almond and Sydney Verba, believe that this "informed" but idle state of the American public is indeed the desired state for sake of stability and the effective working of the government. Proponents of the term limits at the state level seem to be working hard to change this prevailing attitude through various means of communication. The huge bulk of their activities is evidenced by a simple examination of the Internet.

So, for good or for bad, term limits is already a significant item of the American political reality that cannot be ignored by vote-seeking politicians. Even without formal restrictions, some politicians have already been forced to devise their electoral campaign strategy, to provide a reasonable explanation for why the public should continue to support them even though they have already served more than two or three terms. Some, most notably the ones who challenged term limits in courts, even go back on their initial promise to the voters to serve for only two terms. They served, and gradually they become fond of their political post and thus want to stay longer. Interestingly, such bold reneging on oral and even written commitments to quit after their terms are over does not prevent those people from believing that they will not be penalized at the voting booths—so strong is the belief in the power of the incumbency. In fact, party organization loyalists have stood behind this bold public abridging of early commitment.

Moreover, our analysis of the incumbent spatial advantage in chapter 3 showed that by adopting a median strategy, both candidates would present a more or less identical position over policy issues. In this event, voters differentiate between the candidate on the basis of personal attributes: experience, credibility, looks, articulation, and so on. In fact, many electoral campaigns are intentionally designed so that voters will be exposed only to the candidate's personal attributes. Positions on policy issues, those that are important to the voters, are tactically blurred and presented in an ambiguous double-talk form or completely ignored (Doron 1996). It seems, then, that in the age of mass electronic media, where face-to-face interactions are largely an obsolete method of politicking, what become important are the appearances, the images, and the style of delivery (including the body language) of the candidates, not the substance of their messages. Experienced professional strategists can easily adjust to this kind of situation. Based on surveys' findings of voters' preferences, they design costume-made "substantive packages" in which the candidate's personality, and not what he or she stands for, is the central component. Where smiles become more important than the essence of the [Lewis Carroll's] cat, highly exposed performers and even pleasant-looking individuals have a competitive political edge, so it seems, over "plain" imaged candidates.

Term limits somewhat curtail this basis of superficiality upon which people make their choices. It can serve as a tiebreaker of sorts between two strategically designed packages. It introduces another type of consideration of the candidate's attributes, one that can help distinguish between those who have served several terms and new candidates. It enables voters to stop "the show" after only two or three terms of appearance. It cannot, however, prevent the appearances of new showmen and showwomen to replace the veteran players, but at least it opens the chances to other types of candidates to enter the competition. Increasing the chances of being elected is what is expected of an effective democratic competition.

Would Term Limits Change the Quality of Public Policymaking?

Rational expectations would dictate that when people act to obtain something, in this case a restrictive regulation to be imposed on politicians, they expect the outcomes to be better and not worse. Could term limits improve the quality of public policymaking in America for the benefits of the citizens? The answer to this question is of a most practical importance. For if the imposition of term limits on the state and federal level do not improve the quality of policymaking, then the benefits of the reform would amount to a mere replacement of insiders by outsiders. In such a case, the public need not hang high hopes on the political performance of the novice. These novices would then have to be perceived as a group of clever politicians using the public's mounting frustration toward the representatives in order to acquire political posts for themselves. Soon, as has already been revealed in some places, the newly elected politicians will adopt the modes of behavior and practices of the old ones. They become fond of the payoffs obtained from their political positions and act to prolong their personal fortune in violation of their early commitments to the public. If so, then, term limits need not be perceived as an essential or even interesting political reform. But it is.

In a dynamic political context it is difficult to address the question of quality of public policy. Often, good or bad policies are matters for post-priori evaluation. Usually, we know only in retrospect if the policy decisions that were made were effective and that they obtained the agreed-upon goals; usually we cannot know in real time if mistakes in judgment were made. Had we known ahead of time that the consequences of our policies would yield adverse results, we would presumably take the proper corrective measures. However, as Barbara Tuchman has so convincingly demonstrated (1983), this is often not the case. Indeed, policymakers may recognize imminent problems or even potential catastrophes and do little to prevent them. Perhaps the sunk costs involved in significant policy decisions or the powers of inertia are sufficient barriers to necessary correction. In addition, the inability to judge the consequences of the implementation of a given policy ahead of time is partly a direct outcome of the luck of experimentation that should take place prior to the decision to enact that policy (Campbell and Jullian 1966). Even a careful experimentation or a comparative examination of data would not always assure success, as shown in the 1960s busing policy and in other cases. Moreover, often the decision of one person, which is of course difficult to predict in the context of democratic voting, may affect policies in a direction and magnitude that alters history. Thomas Jefferson's position on constitutional matters is a case in point (Riker 1996). Therefore, it cannot be said with much credence that introduction of new politicians will affect the quality of the policies one way or another. We could expect, however, that the new people would design different policies.

Term limits will change the composition of the representatives. No one seriously argues that even in the long run, similar people, members of the same social class, will enter politics post-term limits. Most proponents (and opponents) agree that the new representatives will belong to groups that so far were not able to gain equal representation in the various legislative institutions. Representatives of minority groups (including women) are the likely candidates. These would certainly affect public policy in a direction compatible with the interests of members of their groups, or at least in a direction that would not contradict these interests. For example, while it could easily be shown that market economy first benefits the well-to-do, it would be similarly easy to expect that a minority-based legislature will support laws aiming to correct market failures, failures that could account for the socio-economic inferiority of their groups. Thus, opening the gates of the legislative institutions by way of competition over open seats will alter the substance of public policy. Whether this is a positive or negative development will be determined in retrospect.

What Is the Likelihood for Federal Level Term Limits?

Term limits is a simple and quite catchy populist idea. Once it was introduced into the American political agenda it accumulated momentum, progressing and diffusing the innovation to states (mainly mid-western and western) that seemed to be more easily adaptive to change. Its simplicity has kept it attractive in the eyes of its supporters for a long time. The political entrepreneurs who promote the idea do not fail to package it in sound and attractive reasoning. They argue that not only is it an efficient political solution for an ineffective democracy, but also that most of Founding Fathers held the exact position—as if a non-supporter would change his or her mind because of such facts.

The political people who oppose term limits and their supporters are often being perceived, following a well-publicized term limits campaign, to be sticking to their chairs. This is not only not a very nice position to be in, it also forces them to address in their own campaigns the reasons for their decisions to prolong their stay in government. Such antidotes may or may not be effective. According to the prevailing American ethos, politicians should be serving the people, on a voluntary basis if possible. They should be citizen-legislators, the ones who come from the people, serve the people, and after some time go back to the people. The prevailing political reality, where the representatives became professional politicians, did not alter that ethos.

Term limits is but one sound interpretation of this ethos. It is a way to obtain it. Because the ethos is rooted in the "glorious" past, the ambition to reinstate it is painted with a conservative flair. The logic that underlies it is, however, neither Republican nor Democratic. For in "open seats" races, both parties hold an equal chance of winning a seat. And if so, then, on the average and across the many possible races, *citrus parabus*, the chances of a party that hold a majority to sustain this majority remains unchanged. But there are other ways to interpret this ethos. The third party solution, which attempts to propose changes within the existing political rules of the game, was already mentioned. But a possible solution may point to an alteration of the rules themselves, such as a change from plurality to a proportional representational way of selecting representatives. In such cases, the politicians would face a dilemma: which of the methods proposed to alter politics is the least detrimental to their interests. Term limits may be identified as a method that yields the least damage to their interest; it would thereupon be positively perceived.

But there are two additional arguments that lead us to conclude that in the long run the adaptation of term limits to other states and to the federal level is unavoidable. The first has to do with the internalization of the concept, and the second with the nature of the "new" politicians. While term limits and rotation are very old concepts rooted in the political thinking of the Hebrews and the Greeks, as was shown in chapter 1, its modern formulation is consistent in spirit, if not in logic, with an array of other values that together make for a better polity in a strict Aristotelian sense. Among these values, which relate to both individual and community levels are, for example, responsiveness, accountability, sensitivity, tolerance, and transparency. These are the values that should characterize the normative foundation of a vital civil society operating in a democratic setting. They come in addition to, not instead of, the fundamental democratic values that promote basic freedoms and the protection of individual rights. Their adoption as guidance for collective or private political behavior often comes against resistance from the political system. To illustrate: politicians are usually uncomfortable with a demand for transparency and complete revelation of their public activities (e.g., publicizing the sources of their contributors, or telling what interest groups approach them to represent their case) and therefore may resist attempts to institutionalize this value. Across the board, opposition to this and similar values places the imagined "civil society" against the real political system.

Term limits belong to the set of reforming or "correcting" values, which are part of the set that defines civil society. It encompasses the values of pure motivation, volunteerism, and personal contribution to the public good without corresponding payoff. Given the justified or unjustified argument against the incompetence of the politicians, it is easy to argue why one should be for term limits; it is difficult to defend the status quo. The Supreme Court has done a reasonable job in protecting the status quo, but supporters of term limits are not convinced. Term limits thus have become a concept that has been internalized by many as a "good" value and consequently shapes their political personality. Their future political choices are thus affected one way or another by that value. Hence, whether term limits is a directive, formalized by a set of rules and laws, or a suggestive, in the form of personal or organizational advice to the voters as to how to arrange their preferences, term limits will continue to affect American politics for many years to come.

The second point is somewhat more interesting, even if it contains some speculative elements. The analysis in this book has been conducted in light of our theoretical and empirical knowledge and experience. We referred to political structures and interactive behavior because this is how we usually conduct our analysis. Our strategy is not much different from the way the Court came to decide on the constitutionality of applying term limits to the federal level. The judges made their interpretation and, subsequently, their ruling, based on a historical and legal conceptual construct. We used a different base of knowledge in terms of methodology and assumptions, and therefore our conclusion regarding the same points are different. But what the future of the so-called "information age" entails may make both types of analysis somewhat irrelevant.

For example, with the advances of new electronic technologies and the explosion of information, the new politicians may be quite different from the ones with which we are familiar. Likewise the mode of operation and the substance of our traditional and stable political institution may be quite different. The "Future Shock," to use Alvin Toffler's (1970) quite fitting term, is already here. Concerned voters already have direct and speedy access to all fortresses of power. They already have communities that interact on a regular basis over topics of interest, which are not necessarily the ones politicians are concerned with. More and more, the political agenda is set up outside of Washington by involved citizens. And the process is fast and becoming much faster. Under such conditions, the old breed of politicians seems to be in a relatively disadvantaged position. The old methods of campaigning, either by a direct approach or through the media, and the old supporting organizations (e.g., parties) have become gradually less relevant for political gains. It is not clear what type of skills are necessary to master the world of tomorrow; it is clear, however, that these should be different from the ones used presently. Experience, for example, a highly valued attribute in today's world of politics, may not be so highly valued when the data and knowledge increase at an accelerated rate. From the present point of view, the future uncertainties seem to be too great. Hence, only the ones who can adapt to the new changes would be able to survive the kind of competition the future entails.

It is difficult to believe that when the world moves at a much faster rate than it has been doing in the last several hundred years, politicians will be able to hold up the walls of the fortress for much longer. If they continue to keep the outsiders out by formal legal means, as they currently do, then the reality of the requirement of their "profession" will develop such that either they become irrelevant or they leave their posts voluntarily, just as many did at the formative years of the federation, and for the same reasons: the difficulties and the inconveniences they encounter at the nation's capital. One way or another, term limits will again become the political norm.

Bibliography

Abramowitz, A. I. 1991. "Incumbency, Campaign Spending, and the Decline of Competition in the U.S. House Elections." *Journal of Politics* 53, no. 1: 34-56.

Abramson, Paul, and John Aldrich. 1982. "The Decline of Electoral Participation in America." *The American Political Science Review* 76, no. 3 (September): 502-21.

Abramson, Paul, John Aldrich, Phil Paolino, and David Rohde. 1995. "Third-Party and Independent Candidates in American Politics: Wallace, Anderson and Perot." *Political Science Quarterly* 110, no. 3 (fall): 349-67.

Aldrich, John. 1983. "A Downsian Spatial Model with Party Activism." *American Political Science Review* 77: 974-90.

Alesina, Alberto, and Alex Cukierman. 1990. "The Politics of Ambiguity." *Quarterly Journal of Economics* 105: 829-50.

Alesina, Alberto, and Howard Rosental. 1988. "Partisan Cycles in Congressional Elections and the Macroeconomy." GSIA Working Paper, no. 30-87-88. June.

Almond, Gabriel, and Sydney Verba. 1963. *The Civic Culture*. Princeton: Princeton University Press.

Appleby, Paul. 1949. *Big Democracy*. New York: Knopf.

Aptheker, Herbert. 1976. *Early Years of the Republic*. New York: International Publishers, Inc.

Arrow, Kenneth. 1963. *Social Choice and Individual Values*. New Haven: Yale University Press.

————. 1974. *The Limits of Organizations*. New York: Norton.

Baker, Ross. 1990. "Quack Therapy for Democracy." *Los Angeles Times,* 9 October, B7.

Bandow, Doug. 1996. "The Political Revolution That Wasn't: Why Term Limits Are Needed Now More than Ever." *Policy Analysis*. Cato Policy Analysis, no. 259, September.

Barnard, Chester. 1938. *The Functions of the Executive*. Cambridge: Harvard University Press.

Ben Porth, Yoram. 1975. "The Years of Plenty and the Years of Famine—A Political Business Cycle?" *Kyklos* 28: 400-403.

Benjamin, Gerald, and Michael J. Malbin, eds. 1992. *Limiting Legislative Terms*. Washington D.C.: Congressional Quarterly Inc.

Berkley, George. 1978. *The Craft of Administration*. Boston: Allyn and Bacon.

Berthhoud, John. 1998. "The BBA and Term Limits." *National Taxpayers Union Foundation*. NTU Foundation Issue Brief 101, 6 March.

Black, Duncan. 1958. *The Theory of Committees and Elections*. Cambridge: Cambridge University Press.

Blau, Peter, and Richard Scott. 1962. *Formal Organizations: A Comparative Analysis*. San Francisco: Chandler.

Brams, Steven. 1978. *The Presidential Election Game*. New Haven: Yale University Press.

————. 1985. *Rational Politics: Games and Strategy*. Washington D.C.: Congressional Quarterly Press.

————. 1996. "Presidential Elections American Style." In *The Electoral Revolution*, ed. Gideon Doron. Tel Aviv: Hakibbutz Hameuchad. 79-90.

Brandies, Louis. 1933. *Business: A Profession*. Boston: Small, Maynard.

Braybrook, David, and Charles Lindblom. 1963. *A Strategy of Decision*. New York: Free Press.

Brewster, Lawrence, and Leonard Kooperman. 1997. *A Primer of a California Politics*. New York: St. Martin's Press.

Browne, William P., and Kenneth VerBurg, eds. 1995. *Michigan Politics and Government: Facing Change in a Complex State*. Lincoln, Nebr.: University of Nebraska Press.

Buchanan, James, and Gordon Tallock. 1962. *The Calculus of Consent*. Ann Arbor: University of Michigan Press.

Cain, Bruce, and Marc Levin. 1999. "Term Limits." *Annual Review of Political Science* 2 (June): 163-88.

Campbell, Donald, and Stanley Jullian. 1966. *Experimental and Quasi Experimental Designs for Research.* Chicago: Rand McNally.

Caress, Stanley. 1996. "The Impact of Term Limits on Legislative Behavior: An Examination of a Transitional Legislature." *Political Science & Politics* 29 (December): 671-78.

Carey, John. 1998. *Term Limits and Legislative Representation.* London: Cambridge University Press.

Carey, John, Richard Niemi, and Lynda Powell. 1998. "The Effects of Term Limits on State Legislators." *Legislative Studies Quarterly* 23: 271-300.

———. 1999. *Term Limits in State Legislators.* Ann Arbor: University of Michigan Press.

Cole, Donald B. 1993. *The Presidency of Andrew Jackson.* Lawrence, Kans.: University Press of Kansas.

Colleman, James. 1966. *Equality and Educational Opportunity.* Washington D.C.: U.S. Government Printing Office.

Coyne, James, and John Fund. 1992. *Cleaning House: America's Campaign for Term Limits.* Washington D.C.: Regency.

Crane, Edward, and Roger Pilon, eds. 1994. *The Politics and Law of Term Limits.* Washington D.C.: Cato Institute.

Cronin, Thomas. 1990. "Term Limits—A Symptom, Not a Cure." *New York Times,* 23 December, E11.

Crozier, Morris. 1964. *The Bureaucratic Phenomenon.* London: Tavistock.

Cyret, Richard, and James March. 1963. *The Behavioral Theory of the Firm.* New Jersey: Prentice-Hall.

Demeyer, Frank, and Charles Plott. 1970. "The Probability of Cyclical Majority." *Econometrica* 38: 345-54.

Detweiler, George. 1996. "Term Limits Temptation." *New American* 12, no. 12 (June 10): 23-30.

Donovan, Todd, and Joseph R. Snipp. 1994. "Support for Legislative Term Limitations in California: Group Representation, Partisanship, and Campaign Information." *The Journal of Politics* 56, no. 2: 492-501.

Doron, Gideon. 1986. *To Decide and to Implement.* Rechuvot: Kivunim.

———. 1988. *Rational Politics in Israel.* Tel Aviv: Ramot.

———. 1996. *Strategy of Election.* Rechuvot: Kivunim.

————, ed. 1996. *The Electoral Revolution: Direct Election to the Prime Minister and Primaries*. Tel Aviv: Hakibbutz Hameuchad.

————. 1998. "Public Opinion Polls as an Instrument for Electoral Strategy and Public Policy." In *Truth and Survey*, ed. Camil Fuchs and Bar Lev Shaul. Tel Aviv: Hakibbutz Hameuchad.

Doron, Gideon, and Michael Harris. 2000. *Electoral Reform and Public Policy: The Case of Israel*. Lanham, Md.: Lexington Books.

Doron, Gideon, and Moshe Maor. 1991. "Barriers to Entry Into a Political System: A Theoretical Framework and Empirical Application from the Israeli Experience." *Journal of Theoretical Politics* 3, no 2. 175-88.

Doron, Gideon, and Uri On. 1983. "Evaluating Slack in Public Programs by the Experience Curve Method." In *Evaluating the Welfare State*, ed. Shimon Spiro and Yuchtman-Yaar Ephraim. New York: Academic Press, 255-77.

Doron, Gideon, and Itai Sened. 2001. *Political Bargaining*. London: Sage.

Doron, Gideon, and Daniella Shoncker. 1998. *Awaiting Representation: Women Politics in Israel*. Tel Aviv: Hakibbutz Hameuchad.

Doron, Gideon, and Boaz Tamir. 1983. "The Electoral Cycle: A Political Economic Perspective." *Crossroad* 10 (spring).

Downs, Anthony. 1957. *An Economic Theory of Democracy*. New York: Harper and Row.

————. 1967. *Inside Bureaucracy*. Boston: Little, Brown.

Easton, David. 1953. *The Political System*. New York: Knopf.

Enelow, James, and Melvin Hinich, eds. 1990. *Advances in Spatial Theory of Voting*. New York: Cambridge University Press.

Evans, Diana. 1996. "Before the Roll Call: Interest Group Lobbying and Public Policy Outcomes in House Committees." *Political Research Quarterly* 49: 287-304.

Fayol, Henry. 1987. "General Principles of Management." In *Classics of Administration Theory*, ed. Jay Shafritz and Ott Steven. Chicago: The Dorsey Press, 51-66.

Feldman, Ofer. 2000. *The Japanese Political Personality: Analyzing the Motivations and Culture of Freshman Diet Members*. Houndmills, Basingstoke, Hampshire: Macmillan Press; New York: St. Martin's Press (in association with International Political Science Association).

Fenno, Richard. 1978. *Home Style: House Members in their Districts*. Glenview, Ill.: Scott, Foresman.

Ferguson, James. 1974. *Advertising and Competition: Theory Measurement, Fact.* Cambridge: Brillinger.

Ferry, Jonathan. 1994. "Women, Minorities and Term Limits: America's Path to a Representative Congress." *Term Limits Outlook Series,* Washington, D.C.: U.S. Term Limits Foundation 3, no. 2 (July).

Fiorina, Morris. 1989. *Congress: Keystone of Washington Establishment.* New Haven: Yale University Press.

————. 1992. *Divided Government.* New York: MacMillan.

Frohlich, Norman, Joe Oppenheimer, and Oran Young. 1971. *Political Leadership and Collective Goods.* Princeton: Princeton University Press.

Fund, John. 1992. "Term Limitation: An Idea Whose Time Has Come." *Policy Analysis No. 141* Washington D.C.: Cato Institute, October 30, 1991. In *Limiting Legislative Terms,* ed. Gerald Benjamin and Michael J. Malbin. Washington D.C.: Congressional Quarterly Inc, 225-39.

Goodman, Paul, and Johannes Pennings, eds. 1977. *New Perspectives on Organizational Effectiveness.* San Francisco: Josey Bass.

Goodnow, Frank. 1900. *Politics and Administration.* New York: Russell and Russell.

Goodwin, Doris Kearns. 1994. *No Ordinary Time: Franklin and Eleanor Roosevelt: The Home Front in World War II.* New York: Simon & Schuster.

Gordon, Dianna. 1994. "Citizen Legislators—Alive and Well." *State Legislatures* 20, 1 (January): 24-27.

Grofman, Bernard, ed. 1996. *Legislative Term Limits: Public Choice Perspectives.* Amsterdam: Kluwer.

Gulick, Luther. 1987. "Notes on the Theory of Organizations." In *Classics of Administration Theory,* ed. Jay Shafritz and Steven Ott. Chicago: The Dorsey Press, 87-97.

Gulick, Luther, and L. Urwick, eds. 1937. *Papers on the Science of Administration.* New York: Institute of Public Administration.

Gurr, Robert. 1970. *Why Men Rebel.* Princeton: Princeton University Press.

Hamilton, Alexander, John Jay, and James Madison. 1991. *The Federalist.* Essay 37, ed. Edward M. Earle. New York: Modern Liberty. First published in 1788. In Vincent Ostrom, *The Meaning of American Federalism Constituting a Self-Governing Society.* San Francisco, Calif.: Institute for Contemporary Studies, 103 104.

Harrington, James. 1656. *Commonwealth of Oceana*. London: J. Streater for Livewell Chapman.

Harrington, Katie, and Mary Tolman, 1998. "The Impact of Term Limits on the House Seniority System: An Analysis of the 104th U.S. House." *The Yale Political Quarterly* 20, no. 2 (December).

Hayek, F. A. 1979. *Law, Legislation and Liberty,* Vol. 3. Chicago: University of Chicago Press.

Hibbs, Douglas. 1977. "Political Parties and Macroeconomic Policy." *American Political Science Review* 71 (December): 1467-87.

Hinckley, Barbara. 1971. *The Seniority System in the Congress.* Bloomington: Indiana University Press.

Hirshman, Albert. 1970. *Exit, Voice and Loyalty.* Cambridge: Harvard University Press.

Hirschmann, W. 1964. "Profit from Learning Curve." *Harvard Business Review* 42: 125-39.

Hodson, Timothy, Rich Jones, Karl Kurtz, and Gary Moncrief. 1995. "Leaders and Limits: Changing Patterns of State Legislative Leadership under Term Limits." *Spectrum: The Journal of State Government* 68, no. 3 (summer): 6-15.

Holman, Kwame. 1997. "Serving Time." *Online Newshour.* 12 February.

Hume, David. 1752. "Idea of a Perfect Commonwealth." *Political Discourses.* Edinburgh: R. Fleming.

Hyink, Bernard L., and David H. Provost. 1998. *Politics and Government in California.* Ontario, Canada: Addison-Wesley Publishers.

Jacobson, Gary C. 1993. "Misallocation of Resources in House Campaigns." In *Congress Reconsidered,* 5th ed., ed. Lawrence Dodd and Bruce Oppenheimer. Washington, D.C.: Congressional Quarterly Press.

Kamber, Victor, Henry Hyde, and Richard Gephardt. 1995. *Given Up on Democracy: Why Term Limits are Bad for America.* New York: Regency.

Kant, Immanuel. 1963. "Perpetual Peace." In Lewis White Beck, ed. and trans., *On History.* Indianapolis: Bobbs-Merrill.

Karp, Jeffrey. 1995. "Explaining Public Support for Legislative Term Limits." *Public Opinion Quarterly* 59: 373-91.

Kesler, Charles R. 1992. "Bad Housekeeping: The Case Against Congressional Term Limitations." *Policy Review* 53: 20-25. In Gerald Benjamin and Michael J. Malbin, eds., *Limiting Legislative Terms.* Washington D.C.: Congressional Quarterly Inc.

King, Gary, and A. Gelman. 1991. "Systematic Consequences of Incumbency Advantage in U.S. House Elections." *American Association of Political Science* 35, no. 1 110-38.

Kook, Rebecca. 1992. "The Politics and Production of Corporate National Identity within Democratic Regimes." Ph.D. thesis. Columbia University.

Krehbiel, Keith. 1991. *Information and Legislative Organization.* Ann Arbor: University of Michigan Press.

Laver, Michael, and Norman Schofield. 1990. *Multiparty Politics.* Oxford: Oxford University Press.

———. 1994. *Multiparty Governments.* Oxford: Oxford University Press.

Lijphart, Arand. 1984. *Democracies.* New Haven, Conn.: Yale University Press.

Lijphart, Arand, and Barnard Grofman, eds. 1984. *Choosing an Electoral System.* New York: Preager.

Lindblom, Charles. 1987. "The Science of Muddling Through." In Jay Shafritz and Albert Hyde, eds. *Classics in Theories of Organization.* Chicago: The Dorsey Press: 263-75.

Lofdahl, Lowell. 1992. "The Case for Term Limits." *Counterpoint* 3, no. 5 (December).

Lowi, Theodore. 1969. *The End of Liberalism.* New York: Norton.

Lynn, Jonathan, and Anthony Jay. 1986. *Yes, Prime Minister: The Diaries of the Right Hon. James Hacker.* London: BBC Publications.

Maisel, L. S. 1990. "The Incumbency Advantage." In *Money, Elections and Democracy,* ed. M. L. Nugent and R. J. Johannes. Boulder, Colo.: Westview Press: 119-42.

Malbin, Michael J. 1992. "Federalists v. Antifederalists: The Term-Limitation Debate at the Founding." In *Limiting Legislative Terms,* ed. Gerald Benjamin and Michael J. Malbin. Washington D.C.: Congressional Quarterly Inc: 53-62.

Mann, Thomas. 1979. *Limiting Presidential and Congressional Terms.* Washington, D.C.: American Enterprise Institute.

———. 1994. "Term Limits: A Bad Idea Whose Time Should Never Come." In *The Politics and Law of Term Limits,* ed. Edward Crane and Roger Pilon. Washington D.C.: Cato Institute, 83-95.

Mansbridge, Jane. 1986. *Why We Lost the ERA.* Chicago: University of Chicago Press.

Maor, Moshe. 1996. "Barriers to Entry in the Selection of Party's Candidates: Barriers Analysis in British Parties." In *The Electoral*

Revolution: Direct Election to the Prime Minister and Primaries, ed. Gideon Doron. Tel Aviv: Hakibbutz Hameuchad, 91-109.

————. 1992. "The Dynamics of Majority Rule: Interparty Politics, Minority Government and Western Europe." Ph.D. thesis, London School of Economics.

March, James, and Herbert Simon. 1987. "Theories of Bureaucracy." In *Classics of Administration Theory*, ed. Jay Shafritz and Steven Ott. Chicago: The Dorsey Press, 146-55.

Marckini, Lisa, John Strat, and Eric Rader. 1999. "Term Limits and Campaign Contribution in the Michigan House of Representatives." Paper delivered at the APSA Annual Meeting, Atlanta (September).

Marder, David. 1974. "The Diplomatic Legacy: Accomplishment to be Assessed for Decades." In The Fall of a President, ed. *Washington Post* staff. New York: Dell, 132-48.

Mayhew, David. 1974. *Congress: The Electoral Connection*. New Haven: Yale University Press.

McCullough, David. 1992. *Truman*. New York: Simon & Schuster.

McKelvy, Richard. 1976. "Intransitivities in Multidimensional Voting Models." *Journal of Economic Behavior* 12: 472-82.

Merton, Robert. 1949. *On Theoretical Sociology*. New York: Free Press.

Mevorach, Baruch. 1987. "Is There a Political Monetary Business Cycle?" *The Journal of Interdisciplinary Economics* 1: 215-23.

Mintz, Alex. 1985. "The Military Industrial Complex: American Concepts and Israeli Realities." *Journal of Conflict Resolution* 29: 623-39.

Mishan, E. J. 1976. *Cost-Benefit Analysis*. New York: Preager.

Mitchell, Cleta. 1990. "The Democratic Case for Term Limits." *The Mainstream Democrat* (December).

Moncrief, Gary F., and Joel A. Thompson, eds. 1992. *Changing Patterns in State Legislative Careers*. Ann Arbor: University of Michigan Press.

Moore, Stephen, and Aaron Steelman. 1994. "An Antidote to Federal Red Ink: Term Limits." *Cato Briefing Papers,* no. 21 (November).

Nachmias, David. 1981. "The Role of Evaluation in Public Policy." In *Evaluating and Optimizing Public Policy*, ed. Dennis Palumbo, Stephan Fawcett, and Paula Wright. Lanham, Md.: Lexington Books.

Nash, John. 1950. "The Bargaining Problem." *Econometrica* 18:155-62.

The National Election Studies. 1999. "The NES Guide to Public Opinion and Electoral Behavior." www.umich.edu/~nes/guide/toptable //tab5b_3.html (14 September).

Nelson, Philip. 1974. "The Economic Value of Advertising." In *Advertising and Society*, ed. Y. Brozen. New York: New York University Press, 44-62.

Niemi, Richard, and Herbert Weisberg. 1968. "A Mathematical Solution for the Probability of the Paradox of Voting." *Behavioral Science* 13: 317-23.

Niskanan, William. 1971. *Bureaucracy and Representative Government.* Chicago: Aldine-Alterton.

Nordlinger, Eric. 1970. *Conflict Regulation in Divided Societies.* Cambridge: Harvard University Press.

North, Robert. 1968. "Conflict: Political Aspects." In *International Encyclopedia of the Social Sciences*, ed. David Shills. New York: Free Press.

Norton, Augustus, ed. 1995. *Civil Society in the Middle East.* New York: Brill.

Olson, Mancur. 1965. *The Logic of Collective Action.* Cambridge, Mass.: Harvard University Press.

Ordeshook, Peter. 1986. *Game Theory and Political Theory.* Cambridge: Cambridge University Press.

Ornstein, Norman. 1990. "Only Bums Will Run, Only Bums Will Rule." *Los Angeles Times.* 13 November, B11.

Paine, Thomas. 1776. *Common Sense.* Philadelphia: W. and T. Bradford.

Palumbo, Dennis, and Steven Maynard-Moody. 1991. *Contemporary Public Administration.* New York: Longman.

Parenti, Michael. 1988. *Democracy for the Few.* New York: St. Martin's Press.

Payne, James. 1991a. *The Culture of Spending: Why Congress Lives Beyond Our Means.* San Francisco: ICS Press.

———. 1991b. "Why Government Spending Grows." *Western Political Quarterly* 44: 487-508.

Peretz, Don, and Gideon Doron. 1997. *Government and Politics of Israel.* Boulder, Colo.: Westview Press.

Pérez-Peña, Richard. 1999. "Lawyers Abandon Legislatures for Greener Pastures." *New York Times.* 21 February, sec. 4: 3.

Peters, Guy. 1989. *The Politics of Bureaucracy.* New York: Longman.

Petracca, Mark. 1992a. "Why Political Scientists Oppose Term Limits." *Briefing Papers.* CATO Institute, no. 14, February.

———. 1992b. "Rotation in Office: The History of an Idea." In *Limiting Legislative Terms*, ed. G. Benjamin and M. J. Malbin. Washington, D.C.: Congressional Quarterly, 19-52.

Polsby, Nelson. 1991a. "Constitutional Mischief: What's Wrong with Term Limitations." *The American Prospect* no. 6 (summer): 40-43.
―――. 1991b. "Some Arguments Against Congressional Term Limitations." *Harvard Journal of Law and Public Policy* 16: 63-111.
Pound, William. 1992. "State Legislative Careers: Twenty-Five Years of Reform." In *Changing Patterns in State Legislative Careers*, ed. Gary F. Moncrief and Joel A. Thompson. Ann Arbor: University of Michigan Press.
Powell, J. Bingham. 1982. *Contemporary Democracies: Participation, Stability and Violence*. Cambridge: Harvard University Press.
―――. 1986. "American Voter Turnout in Comparative Perspective." *American Political Science Review* 80: 17-43.
Quandt, Willam. 1986. *Camp David: Peacemaking and Politics*. Washington, D.C.: Brookings.
―――. 1993. *Peace Process*. Washington, D.C.: Brookings.
Rae, Douglas. 1967. *The Political Consequences of Electoral Laws*. New Haven: Yale University Press.
Redford, Emmette. 1958. "The Neverending Search for the Public Interest." In *Ideal and Practice in Public Administration*, ed. Emmette Redford. University, Ala.: University of Alabama Press.
Remini, Robert V. 1981. *Andrew Jackson and the Course of American Freedom, 1822-1832*, Vol. II. New York: Harper & Row.
Riker, William. 1969. "Arrows Theorem and Some Examples of the Paradox of Voting." In *Mathematical Applications in Political Science*, ed. John Claunch. Dallas: Southern Methodist University Press.
―――. 1980. "Implication of the Disequilibrium of Majority Rule for the Study of Institutions." *American Political Science Review* 74: 432-46.
―――. 1982. *Liberalism Against Populism*. San Francisco: Freeman.
―――. 1986. *The Art of Political Manipulation*. New Haven: Yale University Press.
―――. 1996. *The Strategy of Rhetoric: Campaigning for the American Constitution*. New Haven: Yale University Press.
Riker, William, and Steven Brams. 1973. "The Paradox of Vote Trading." *The American Political Science Review* 67, no.4 (December): 1235-47.
Riker, William, and Peter Ordeshook. 1973. *An Introduction to Positive Political Theory*. New Jersey: Prentice-Hall.

Ripley, Randall. 1988. *Congress: Process and Policy*. New York: W.W. Norton.

Rose, Richard. 1984. "Electoral Systems: A Question of Degree or Principle?" In *Choosing an Electoral System*, ed. Arand Lijphart and Barnard Grofman. New York: Preager.

Rosenthal, Alan. 1998. *The Decline of Representative Democracy: Process, Participation, and Power in State Legislatures*. Washington, D.C.: Congressional Quarterly Press.

Rotunda, Ronald. 1995. "Term Limits and Lessons From Our Past." *Heartland Policy Study*. Chicago: The Heartland Institute (June).

Sabato, Larry. 1984. *PAC Power: Inside the World of Political Action Committees*. New York: Norton.

Sarbaugh-Thompson, Marjorie, and Lyke Thompson. 1999. "Webs of Influence: Predicted Relationships Among Legislators in Term Limited State House." Paper delivered at the APSA Annual Meeting, Atlanta (September).

Sargent, T. J., and N. Wallace. 1976. "Rational Expectations and the Theory of Economic Policy." *Journal of Monitory Economics* (April): 169-84.

Schrag, Peter. 1995. "The Populist Road To Hell." *The American Prospect* 24 (Winter): 24-30.

Seligman, Adam. 1992. *The Idea of Civil Society*. New York: Free Press.

Selznick, Philip. 1966. *TVA and the Grass Roots*. New York: Harper.

Sen, Amartya. 1970. *Collective Choice and Social Welfare*. San Francisco: Holden Day.

Shafritz, Jay, and Albert Hyde, eds. 1987. *Classics in Theories of Organization*. Chicago: The Dorsey Press.

Shafritz, Jay, and Steven Ott, eds. 1987. *Classics of Administration Theory*. Chicago: The Dorsey Press.

Shepsle, Kenneth, and Mark Bonchek. 1997. *Analyzing Politics: Rationality, Behavior and Institutions*. New York: W.W. Norton.

Shepsle, Kenneth, and Barry Weingast. 1981. "Structure Induced Equilibrium and Legislative Choice." *Public Choice* 37: 503-19.

Simon, Herbert. 1967. *Administrative Behavior*. 3d ed. New York: Free Press.

———. 1987. "The Proverbs of Administration." In *Classics of Administration Theory*, ed. Jay Shafritz and Steven Ott. Chicago: The Dorsey Press, 102-19.

Sims, C. A. 1983. "Is There an Economic Business Cycle?" *The American Economic Review* 73 (May): 228-33.

Steelman, Aaron. 1998. "The Limits Rattle Politicians." *Investor's Business Daily.* 11 November: A1, A24.

Steiner, Peter. 1977. "The Public Sector and the Public Interest." In *Public Expenditures and Policy Analysis*, ed. Richard Haveman and Julius Margolis. New York: Rand McNally, 27-66.

Stigler, George. 1971. "The Theory of Economic Regulation." *Bell Journal of Economics* (spring): 137-46.

Stillman II, Richard J. 1991. *Preface to Public Administration: A Search for Themes and Direction.* New York: St. Martin's Press.

Strom, Kaare. 1984. "Minority Government in Parliamentary Democracies: The Rationality of Non-Wining Cabinet Solution." *Comparative Studies* 17:199-227.

———. 1990. *Minority Government and Majority Rule.* Cambridge: Cambridge University Press.

Tabarrok, Alexander. 1994. "A Survey, Critique, and New Defense of Term Limits." *The Cato Journal* 14, no. 2 (fall): 333-50.

Taylor, Fredrick. 1911. *Scientific Management.* New York: Harper.

Taylor, J. B. 1983. "Rational Expectations and the Invisible Handshake." In *Macroeconomics, Prices and Quantities*, ed. James Tobin. Washington D.C.: The Brookings Institution.

Thompson, James D., and William J. McEwen. 1958. "Organizational Goals and Environment: Goal Setting and Interaction Process." *American Sociological Review* 23, no. 1 (February): 23-31.

Tocqeville de, Alexis. 1944. *Democracy in America* (2 vols.) ed. Bradly Phillips. New York: Knopf.

Toffler, Alvin. 1970. *Future Shock.* New York: Random House.

Tuchman, Barbara. 1983. *The March of Folly: From Troy to Vietnam.* New York: Knopf.

Tufte, Edward. 1978. *Political Control of the Economy.* Princeton: Princeton University Press.

Tullock, Gordon. 1967. *Toward a Mathematics of Politics.* Ann Arbor: University of Michigan Press.

U.S. Term Limits. "About USTL – Mission." www.termlimits.org/About /about.html (15 June 2000).

U.S. Term Limits, Inc. v. Thornton. 1995. 115 S. Ct. 1842.

Walton, Richard. 1980. "Up Against the Ballot: The Two-Party Monopoly." *Nation* 231, no. 6: 176-78.

Washington Post. 1997. 17 June, A4.

Weber, Max. 1958. "Bureaucracy." In *From Max Weber: Essays in Sociology*, ed. Hans Gerth and C. Wright Mills. New York: Oxford University Press, 196-244.

Wildavsky, Aaron. 1974. *The Politics of the Budgetary Process*. Boston: Little, Brown.

———. 1988. *The New Politics of the Budgetary Process*. Glenview, Ill.: Scott, Foresman.

Will, George. 1991. *Restoration: Congress, Term Limits and the Recovery of Deliberative Democracy*. New York: Free Press.

———. 1997a. "Limiting Terms of Office for Members of the U.S. Senate and U.S. House of Representatives." Testimony to the House Subcommittee on Term Limits, 22 January.

———. 1997b. "A Congressional Raise—For Term Limits." *Washington Post*. 12 June, A23.

Wilson, James. 1982. "The Rise of the Bureaucratic State." In *Current Issues in Public Administration*, ed. Fredrick Lane. New York: St. Martin's Press.

Wilson, Woodrow. 1887. "The Study of Administration." *Political Science Quarterly* 2, no. 2 (June): 197-222.

Yuchtman, Ephraim, and Stenly Seashore. 1967. "A System Resource Approach to Organizational Effectiveness." *American Sociological Review* 32: 891-903.

Zuckerman, Alan. 1990. "The Flow of Vote in Israel: Reconsideration of Stability and Change." In *The Elections in Israel: 1998*, ed. Asher Arian and Michal Shamir. Boulder, Colo.: Westview, 189-201.

Index

About the Authors

Gideon Doron is one of Israel's best-known experts on public policy. He is on the faculty of the department of political science at Tel Aviv University and on the faculty of the department of public policy at Ben Gurion University in Israel. He has published twelve books and numerous articles on such topics as political bargaining, barriers to entry into Israeli politics, and election strategies. Gideon Doron received his bachelor's degree in political science and interdepartmental studies and his master's degree in political science and public administration from the Hebrew University in Jerusalem. He received another master's degree and a Ph.D. in political science from the University of Rochester in New York.

Michael Harris specializes in public policy and public administration. He is a professor of political science and is currently serving as the Associate Vice President for Academic Affairs at Eastern Michigan University. His work has been published in a variety of journals. Harris has been recognized for excellence in teaching by the American Political Science Association and was awarded the Michigan Association of Governing Boards Distinguished Faculty Award. Harris has acted as a political commentator to the ABC and FOX local affiliates as well as Israeli television. Michael Harris received his undergraduate degree in economics and business administration from Bar-Ilan University. He received his master's degree from Tel-Aviv University and his Ph.D. in public policy from Indiana University.